DR. KALAM'S PURA MODEL AND SOCIETAL TRANSFORMATION

DR. KALAM'S PURA MODEL AND SOCIETAL TRANSFORMATION

Edited by

P. JEGADISH GANDHI
Founder-Director,
Vellore Institute of Development Studies (VIDS),
Sathuvachari, Vellore

DEEP & DEEP PUBLICATIONS PVT. LTD.
F-159, Rajouri Garden, New Delhi-110027

DR. KALAM'S PURA MODEL AND
SOCIETAL TRANSFORMATION

ISBN 81-7629-664-3

Typeset by PRINT INDIA, A-38/2, Phase I, Mayapuri, New Delhi-110064.

Printed in India at ELEGANT PRINTERS, A-38/2, Phase I, Mayapuri, New Delhi-110064.

Published by DEEP & DEEP PUBLICATIONS PVT. LTD.,
F-159, Rajouri Garden, New Delhi-110027. Phones: 25435369, 25440916.
E-mail: deep98@del3.vsnl.net.in

Sales Showroom: 2/13, Ansari Road, Daryaganj, New Delhi-110002
Phone/Fax: 23245122

To

Dr. Manmohan Singh,

the First Economist-

Prime Minister of India

Contents

PART III

POST-PURA SCENARIO: TRANSFORMING RURAL "REALITIES"

Preface

Rural development is not only a process, a method, a programme, but also a movement in our country. Ever since Dr. A.P.J. Abdul Kalam has become President of India (July 25, 2002), he has spearheaded a socio-economic movement of igniting the young minds with positive thoughts and of propagating the "Developed India by 2020" vision with constructive mission modes. As President, for the first time, Dr. Kalam has outlined his pet project of PURA—Providing Urban Amenities in Rural Areas in the book release function held at the Nehru Memorial Museum, New Delhi on October 23, 2002. Since then, Dr. Kalam has passionately championing for the PURA scheme to be implemented as part of 'Developed India' vision in almost all his Presidential addresses and social dialogues. His persuasive advocacy has convinced the then Prime Minister, A.B. Vajpayee to declare a policy pronouncement in his Independence Day Address on August 15, 2003 that PURA as the NDA government—propelled rural project. This has kindled many state governments, private organizations and NGOs to direct their efforts towards creating more PURAs which are economically viable and technologically sustainable. The United Progressive Alliance (UPA) under the Prime Ministership of Dr. Manmohan Singh has adopted pro-PURA approach as part of "New Deal" for rural India. As NGO consultant on rural development programmes, I feel that the connectivity mechanism embedded in PURA is a pragmatic approach for rural regeneration and urban renewal.

The New Indian Express has published as part of my letter to the Prime Minister of India under the news caption, "Manmohan urged to revitalize reforms" (May 26, 2004) as follows:

> "Conveying his greetings to the new Prime Minister, Gandhi said rural development is the catalyst to attain all-round growth. Alternative rural development programmes like Providing Urban Amenities in Rural Areas (PURA), as announced by the NDA government and endorsed by President A.P.J. Abdul Kalam, were there to develop 5,000 rural cluster areas in the country.... This PURA model must be continued, adding that the Prime Minister should help usher in a new societal transformation."

After publishing my book on *The Socio-Economic Thoughts of A.P.J. Abdul Kalam* in February 2004, I have got very encouraging response from the academic circles all over India and critical book reviews in leading newspapers and journals. Today, Dr. Kalam's PURA Scheme is being discussed in all forums, such as seminars, symposia and workshops, be it in universities, colleges, research institutes, government policy bodies or the ones organized by private enterprises. To understand the dialects and dynamics of PURA programme in proper perspective, I collated the available materials and put them under the title *Dr. Kalam's PURA Model and Societal Transformation* for the benefit of academic and non-academic communities.

I record my grateful thanks to His Excellency the President of India, Dr. A.P.J. Abdul Kalam for his "no objection permission to a quote from the published literature and the published books of the President."

When I conceived the contents of the book, immediately my memory lane goes down to the copious elucidatory critical inputs on PURA seralised in *The Hindu-Business Line* by Dr. P.V. Indiresan, former Director of the Indian Institute of Technology, Chennai, now residing at New Delhi. In complying with my request, he has not only given approval to reproduce his published papers, but also sent, admist his busy travelling schedule, a valuable special introduction. *This forms the first part of Introduction to my book.* I am highly indebted to him for the fine gesture of encouragement in my academic venture.

I owe a great deal to Dr. K. Venkatasubramanian, former Member, Planning Commission, Government of India, for his initial inspirational guidance to do research into the socio-economic thoughts of Dr. Kalam.

As Life member of the 86-year old Indian Economic Association, I had the privilege of attending many annual conferences and developed good academic fellowship with eminent economists and great teachers in Economics from different parts of the country. Among them many are my well-wishers. I record my sincere thanks to Prof. Ruddar Datt, Past President of the Indian Economic Association and author of the popular text book, *Indian Economy*, for his valuable contribution to this volume.

Thanks are due to Mr. L. Pradeep Kumar, SLN Xerox Sathuvachari, Vellore, for is sincere work at Computer in processing the typed materials.

Special thanks are due to my wife, Sugirtham, daughters —Shobhana, Deepa and Mary Isaac, son-in-law, Isaac Deva Kumar and grandson, Jonathan Charles (Joe) for their constant moral support in all my academic sojourns.

This publication would not have been possible without the cordial cooperation of Mr. G.S. Bhatia, Deep and Deep Publications Pvt. Ltd., New Delhi.

P. JEGADISH GANDHI

Acknowledgements

Special thanks are due to the Editors, *The Hindu-Business Line, The Hindu, and The New Sunday Express* for their published materials which form the major contents of this book.

P. JEGADISH GANDHI

Abbreviations

NGOs	—	Non-Government Organisations
UPA	—	United Progressive Alliance
PURA	—	Providing Urban Amenities in Rural Areas
MSSRF	—	M.S. Swaminathan Research Foundation
VRC	—	Village Resource Centre
IT	—	Information Technology
ISRO	—	Indian Space Research Organisation
IMM 2020	—	India Millennium Mission 2020
R&D	—	Research & Development
ITU	—	International Telecommunication Union
DAI	—	Digital Access Index
ICT	—	Information and Communication Technology
UNCTAD	—	United Nations Conference on Trade and Development
UMI	—	Upper Middle Income
NCMP	—	National Common Minimum Programme
ITI	—	Industrial Training Institute
NDA	—	National Democratic Alliance
TIFAC	—	Technology Information Forecasting and Assessment

UNDP	— United Nations Development Programme
IIT	— Indian Institute of Technology
DRDO	— Defence Research and Development Organisation
CSIR	— Central Scientific and Industrial Research
CMD	— Central Managing Director
CEO	— Chief Executive Officer
HUDCO	— Housing and Urban Development Corporation of India
TV	— Television
CSR	— Corporate Social Responsibility
USP	— Usual Principal Status
GDP	— Gross Domestic Product
URM	— Urban-Rural Migration
RUM	— Rural-Urban Migration
STD	— Subscribers Direct Dialling
PCO	— Personal Call Office
BSNL	— Bharat Sanchar Nigam Limited
SHGs	— Self-Help Groups
NABARD	— National Bank for Agriculture and Rural Development
SRMC	— Sri Ramachandra Medical College
INSAT	— Indian National Satellite
ITC, DYNAMIX, MAHINDRA, TATA EID PARRY, DCM	— Popular Indian Corporates
US	— United States
ICICI	— Industrial Credit and Investment Corporation of India
CICs	— Community Information Centres
PC	— Personal Computer
BPO	— Business Process Outsourcing

Introduction

I

PURA is one of the five major components of President's Dream, his Vision 2020 for a Developed India. It differs from the conventional ideas of economic development of rural areas in six different ways:

(a) It aims at a comprehensive development of rural areas to generate urban-level incomes, and not mere "poverty alleviation".

(b) It plans for an investment at urban levels and not the much lower amounts that prevails at present.

(c) It aims to generate employment for the educated, thereby, halt and even reverse rural-urban migration

(d) It treats quality infrastructure as the prerequisite and not the consequence of development.

(e) It seeks modern industry, investment in social and commercial service instead of rural handicrafts and agri-based small industry.

(f) It relies on private initiative. It is a for-profit enterprise not dependent on subsidy from the government.

Normally, rural development schemes aim to minimise investment; PURA maximises Return-on Investment. While most rural development schemes confine themselves to investment in thousands or, at the most, lakhs of rupees, PURA dreams of hundreds of crores. Economists are understandably exercised about equity and economic disparity but at the individual level. In PURA the concern is about disparity at the macro-level. In the Tenth Five Year Plan, gross investment will be about Rs. 20,000 per capita. At that rate, a typical rural development block should get an investment of Rs. 200 crores, no less. However, while nobody bats an eye lid to spend such sums on flyovers alone in metropolitan cities, they will be shocked to hear of such investments for the total development of a rural block. They fear that rural areas cannot absorb such high levels of investment. PURA aims to prove that, in all fairness, rural areas deserve same levels of investment as cities do; that they can provide better returns on such investment the congested cities can.

PURA is an example of application of technology innovation for development . The tasks of technology are several: Reduce costs of production; offer higher levels of quality and utility; improve ecology; empower less skilled persons to produce more complex artefacts and services, and thereby raise their incomes. PURA satisfies all these conditions.

Because PURA differs from conventional wisdom, the state apparatus has, as yet, no mechanism to implement PURA. It is also threatens the power equation that prevails in villages. PURA has the disadvantage that it has a high starting threshold: One cannot build roads and other infrastructure in small steps. For these reasons, in spite of the President's best efforts, the government has rejected essential elements of PURA, such as, urban level investment, quality services and infusion of private investment and management. Instead, it has appropriated the name PURA for a watered-down version that can by no means fulfil the President's Dream for a Developed India. More education and public pressure are required before PURA can take off.

— *P.V. Indiresan*

II

Rural development is not only a process, a method, a programme, but also a movement in our country. For the past 57 years, the rural-urban divide has become wider in spite of a slew of government and non-governmental development programmes. Problems of poverty, unemployment, deprivation and discrimination are still haunting the rural side.

Dr. Kalam's PURA habitat design has impactionally revolutionised the rural India connecting with the available amenities of urban centres. The book is divided into three parts: Pre-PURA Stage: Socio-economic "divides", The PURA Revolution: Creating "connectivities" and Post-PURA Scenario: Transforming Rural India "Realities". Part I focuses on the dynamics of societal transformation and the dialects of rural-urban divide. Part II discusses Dr. Kalam's PURA model in all its theoretical, analytical, philosophical and practical dimensions. Part III highlights the success stories of PURA in different parts of India.

Dr. S.P. Gupta *et. al.*, in Planning Commission document, *"India Vision 2020"*, have pointed out that a key component for rural development is the provision of roads of connectivity, access being essential for social and economic well-being.

Dr. A.P.J. Abdul Kalam presented his pet PURA model in a simple illustrative style and intelligible language to all people. Knowledge power rural development is an essential need for transforming India into a knowledge superpower. High bandwidth rural connectivity is the minimum requirement to take education, healthcare, and economic dynamism to the rural areas. Providing Urban Amenities in Rural Areas is essentially conceived around four types of connectivities—Physical, Electronic, Knowledge and Economic—with the aim to speed up the process of achieving total rural prosperity. Dr. Kalam has also pointed out that PURA has to be a business proposition which is economically viable and managed by entrepreneurs and small-scale industrialists, as it involves education, health, power generation, transport and management. PURA needs an integrated development approach with empowered management structure.

Dr. P.V. Indiresan's collected essays have been rearranged with subtitles to suit the academic community. He has critically elucidated and evaluated PURA scheme in all its aspects with special focus on its implementational challenges and opportunities. The implementation strategy of PURA visualizes a consortium of promoters to initiate the process by offering to establish in the rural area an export business employing around a thousand workers and a unifier to finalise an economical alignment of a ring road to link a set of villages with the financial investment from the promoters and organisational support from the Government and NGOs. He remarked that in place of doles, PURA tackles rural poverty by generating wage employment. It even hopes to reverse rural-urban migration by attracting high-end jobs that are currently the monopoly of large cities. For that reason PURA will be located near fast expanding cities. That is not as idealistic as going to the most backward of the backward districts but it stands a better chance of success. As villages near cities are more populous, it will still address a large proportion of the rural population.

He has particularised the inherent hurdles to be crossed over in implementing PURA projects—the hesistant profit-induced private investment in the rural areas, the resistant excessive compensation for the surrendered lands from the farmers and the consistent poor demand coupled with low purchasing power of the villagers. In his advocacy for a modified PURA, Dr. Indiresan explained that it will be a useful supplement to the model of PURA i.e., it is more than a plan for "Providing Urban Amenities in Rural Areas"; it is a "Partnership of entrepreneurs, government administrators and the local populace for Urban Amenities within Rural Ambience". In contrast, in the present scheme of PURA, the government proceeds alone; it does not let others have co-ownership.

He is optimistic about the socio-economic viability of PURA with the induction of both organised businesses and their employees. It will see not marginal growth but total transformation, a transformation that will create educated employment with rural areas, curb rural-urban migration and prevent the satanic growth of slum-infested cities. Moreover, it will succeed best when located not far from fast growing cities. This is quite appropriate because, such villages need to grow as much as those in backward areas. Once one PURA takes off, the concept will roll to fill Dr. Kalam's dream.

Prof. Ruddar Datt has brought out the comparative dimensions between the Gandhian model of rural development and the Kalamite PURA model. Yet in the prescription, Dr. Kalam's model is neo-Gandhian in the sense, that it intends to bring rural regeneration with the avowed objective of taking modern technology and modern amenities to the rural areas. In this sense, it does not enter into the controversy of labour-intensive *versus* capital-intensive measures. However, it does emphasize the enlargement of employment as the sole objective to make use of rural manpower in various development activities.

Dr. K. Venkatasubramanian has analysed the uniqueness of the PURA model in five ways: Government contribution is not a grant, but a recoverable investment, public-private partnership, implementation not in the most backward areas, but in the proximity of growing cities; gradual start and spread of rural clusters and ring road connectivity. He advocated that PURA will be implemented not as the usual grant-in-aid rural development scheme, but as a bankable, profit-making, commercial venture.

Dr. M.S. Swaminathan has explained how the Indian Space Research Organisation (ISRO)—M.S. Swaminathan Research Foundation (MSSRF)—Village Resource Centre (VRC) project is working for digital connectivity to remote villages for providing services such as telemedicine, tele-education and remote sensing applications through a single window. Further this programme will concentrate on helping rural women, men and children meet their basic needs in education, nutrition, health, drinking and irrigation water, agriculture and markets. He suggested that a number of expert organisations in agriculture, nutrition, livelihoods, animal husbandry, post-harvest technology, health environmental issues, should be identified to support e-governance programmes.

Mr. S.S. Jeevan, in his on-the-spot survey report, said that something magical is happening in India's Villages. Information Technology (IT) which was once dismissed by cynics as only benefiting the urban elite is fast becoming a developmental tool for India's villagers. From fisherfolk getting vital information on weather alerts in Pondicherry, to shrimp farmers in Andhra Pradesh checking out global price fluctuation, the World Wide Web is touching the lives of villages across India. Virtual villages have come up in different parts of India and the village market is tapped by some big leading companies. He identified that the biggest bottleneck is the lack of political will and imagination. The political classes need to realise that 70 percent of India live in villages, most of whom are still not logged on. If they get wired soon, there is huge political capital to be made from IT-connected villages. Rural empowerment will follow.

In his field study, **Mr. Anand Parthasarathy** found out that Dr. Kalam's vision of taking urban technologies to rural areas is being, realised in a number of "digital divide" projects. His visit to Kuppam's (mean Bangalore) 'inclusive' or i-community shows how the state government as well as a dozen private companies, charitable foundations and non-governmental agencies to come together and co-create a sustainable future for this so-called backward area, using cutting edge technologies that have largely been the preserve of urban pockets of plenty. The challenge remains to sustain the 'inclusive' drive, even while striving to create hundreds of other Kuppams.

In my papers on "Dynamics of Societial Transformation" and "PURA: An Academic Angle," I explained Dr. Kalam's concept of Societal Transformation in terms of his four stages of transition, wealth generation, knowledge incrementalisan and competitiveness and challenges towards a strong India and the PURA Model in statistical and diagrammatical interpretations respectively.

Dr. Kalam's PURA vision model of rural development has now been widely debated and discussed in all forums of nation-building. Some pre-conditions for "take off" for PURA programmes are well laid down in terms of the government recognition, private-philanthropic business initiatives, corporate rural entries, NGOs co-operative gestures, academic and research institutions pioneering efforts and above all, rural peoples' new mind set to partake in the 'digital' dynamics. Now a pro-PURA development culture is catching up. Rural connectivity projects are coming up in various parts of our country. Time is not far off to see Dr. Kalam's PURA dream a reality.

P. JEGADISH GANDHI

List of Contributors

1. **Dr. A.P.J. Abdul Kalam:** The President of India.
2. **Mr. Ananda Parthasarathy:** Reporter, The Hindu.
3. **Dr. S.P. Gupta:** Chairman, The Committee on "India Vision 2020", Planning Commission, Government of India.
4. **Dr. P.V. Indiresan:** Former Director, Indian Institute of Technology, Chennai.
5. **Mr. S.S. Jeevan:** Reporter, The New Sunday Express.
6. **Dr. Ruddar Datt:** Former President, Indian Economic Association, New Delhi.
7. **Dr. M.S. Swaminathan:** Chairman, M.S. Swaminathan Research Foundation, Chennai.
8. **Dr. K. Venkatasubramanian:** Former Member, Planning Commission, Government of India.
9. **Dr. P. Jegadish Gandhi:** The Editor.

PART I

PRE-PURA STAGE: SOCIO-ECONOMIC "DIVIDES"

1

Dynamics of Societal Transformation

P. JEGADISH GANDHI

Social change has occurred in all societies and in all periods of time. But the rate of change differs from society to society. *In Basic Sociological Principles*, Professor Jones said, "Social change is a term used to describe variations in, or modifications of, any aspect of social processes, social patterns, social interaction or social organization." On the other hand, Societal transformation signifies metamorphic changes in shape, form, substance and character of social structural activities. "We have to realise that we are in the age of discontinuity. Things considered almost impossible or most unlikely only 50 years ago have happened" (Vipen Kapur).

POWER OF KNOWLEDGE

Knowledge is the only instrument of production that is not subject to diminishing returns (J.M. Clark, 1927). Humankind can finally place its trust not in a proletarian authoritarianism, not in a secularized humanism, both of which have betrayed the spiritual property right of history, but in a sacramental brotherhood and in the unity of knowledge. This new consciousness has created a widening of human horizons beyond every parochialism, and a revolution in human thought (Ruth Nanda Anshen). The growth of knowledge is one of the most irreversible forces known to mankind. It takes a catastrophe of very large dimensions to diminish the total stock of knowledge in the possession of man (Kenneth E. Boulding). In the 21st century, the most basic of all the raw materials will be knowledge. . . . Knowledge is the most democratic source of power. The control of knowledge is the crux of tomorrow's world wide struggle for power in every human institution (Alvin Toffler, *Power Shift*).

STAGES OF TRANSITION

It is often argued that countries pass through phases during the course of development and that by identifying these stages, according to certain characteristics, a country can be deemed to have reached a certain stage of development. Dr. Kalam in *Ignited Minds* described four stages of transition in a nation's development. His analysis is based on the analogical methodology adopted by Wayne W. Dyer in *Manifest Your Destiny* (1997). The different Stages are : 1. The Athlete Stage, 2. The Warrior Stage, 3. The States Person Stage, and 4. The Self-Realization Stage. He retermed Dyer's the last two stages, statesperson and spirit stages into Big Brother stage and the Self-Realization stage respectively in the discussion of societal transformation.

It is rewarding to reproduce Dr. Kalam's exposition and elucidation: "In the first, *athlete stage,* a nation fresh from an independence struggle, or some other transition, embarks on an energetic pursuit of performance and achievement. This has happened in Japan, Singapore and Malaysia. When a nation leaves this stage behind, it generally enters the *warrior stage*. Proud of its achievements, it finds ways to demonstrate its superiority over others, perhaps through conquest. Ego is the driving force. During this stage people are busy with goals and achievements in competition with others. Convincing others of its superiority becomes the them."

In the next, *big brother stage,* the ego has been tamed somewhat and with its newfound maturity awareness shifts to what is important to other nations and societies. In the big brother stage the nation is still an achiever but it is not so obsessed with proving its strength. The idea is to help other become better. The erstwhile Soviet Union by its development role in some countries had adopted this role. As with the individual, so too with the nation, the transition from the warrior stage to the big brother stage is a rewarding but difficult exercise. There is one stage even higher than this big brother stage. In this, a nation recognizes its truest essence. It comes out of the wisdom that the earth is no single nation's inheritance but of all, and its people are aware of the responsibility of the individual towards his fellow human beings. This can be called *the realization stage*.

Dr. Kalam said that "the stages do not follow in sequence necessarily; they can be coexistent, with one aspect dominant." With the "newfound maturity awareness" that India should become strong and leading nation, "an achiever" in various technological knowledge sectors and big brother attitude towards many Asia-African countries in rebuilding their socio-economic structures, we may describe, India is the third stage of societal transformation. For another two decades, India may strength the base and consolidate the gains of the big brother stage. We may visualize the fourth stage of transition beyond the 'developed India' status by 2020. Kalam is optimistically confident that "India may have the potential to achieve" the realization stage.

Dr. Kalam is totally committed to trigger off a self-reliance movement in India. He has identified Indianization to be the key spirit behind nation-building. It refers to the requirement in individual behaviour patterns so as to maxmimise the achievement for the future in the material and technological spheres. His main postulate here is that if India has to achieve the technological strengths, a self-reliance in Indian products and Indian systems have to grow in the minds of the people. "A nation's progress depends upon how its people think. India has to think as a nation of a billion people."

TRANSFORMATIONAL DEVELOPMENT

Transformational Development is more than just 'change with growth.' 'Transformation may be described as a step higher than development, which in turn, is a step above growth. Growth is purely quantitative; development is both quantitative and qualitative but the person remains the same as before. On the other hand, transformation is like a caterpillar turning into a butterfly' (P.V. Indiresan).

Dr. Kalam's vision of Societal Transformation envisions a simultaneous structural change in the agricultural, industrial, information and knowledge societies based on the fast sectoral sequential value additions. The transformational dynamics will be thus: "The agriculture society concentrated on producing the natural products such as grains, fruits, timber, ores and natural minerals, etc. The industrial society added value to these products by incorporating explicit knowledge (High Technology) to it. This not only added value to products but also increased the productivity. The Information Society adds further value by widely making available the explicit knowledge through electronic networking of information centres and thus making available information products worldwide. The knowledge society will be the society producing products and services that are rich in both explicit and tacit knowledge thus creating more valuable products. It will emerge as a centre of excellence in certain institutions, which will expand to cover the entire country in decade. The leading social group of the knowledge society will be its knowledge workers, who will have sufficient knowledge to create explicit and tacit knowledge rich products. The society will be highly networked to create knowledge intensive environment along with enabling process to efficiently create, share exploit and protect the knowledge. The IT growth in India really has highlighted that it is possible the data transformed into the information has a business proposition. By 2020, India would aim at IT enabled services consisting of human resource service, customer interaction, finance and accounting, data search and integration and remote education. In the coming decades, the enriched young, will see a confluence of civilisational and modern technological streams."

ROAD MAP FOR A STRONG INDIA

"After Independence, India looked forward to development through Five Year Plans. The Green revolution and the technology growth enabled India to attain self-sufficiency in food and have achievements in many technological frontiers particularly during the last two decades. A major transformation came during the information age where India established its position with its strong core competence in Information Technology. Today India is advancing towards the knowledge age which will provide the foundation to become a developed nation with strong economy. A developed country is one which has the capability and the capacity the comprehensively look at wealth generation and wealth protection and thereafter evolve integrated strategies, technologies and missions to meet these objectives. It is also a fact that technology is the established currency of geo-political power and in the Indian context technology has to be the driving force for economical development and national security. India Millennium Mission 2020 (IMM 2020), provides an excellent framework and road-map for making a strong and developed India by the year 2020—the second vision of the Nation." Dr. Kalam is optimistic about that "The Second Vision will bring about a renaissance to the nation. The task of casting a strong India is in the hands of a visionary political leadership."

KNOWLEDGE SOCIETY

"During the last century the world has changed from being an agricultural society, in which manual labour was the critical factor, to an industrial society where the management of technology, capital and labour provide the competitive advantage. In the twenty-first century, a new society is emerging where knowledge is the primary production resource instead of capital and labour. Efficient utilization of this existing knowledge base can create wealth for us in the form of better health, education and other indicators of progress. The ability to create and maintain the knowledge infrastructure, to enhance skills and increase productivity through the exploitation of advance in various fields will be the key factors in deciding the prosperity of this society." Dr. Kalam, in *Ignited Minds* and his *Presidential Speeches* presents a kaleidoscopical picture of the emerging knowledge society in India. Its three focal components are: Societal Transformation, Wealth Generation and Knowledge Incrementalism.

SOCIETAL TRANSFORMATION

The societal transformation is in respect of education, healthcare, agriculture and governance. "These will lead to employment generation, high productivity and rural prosperity. Educational institutions have to gear up to evolve a curriculum that is sensitive to the social and technological needs of developed India. Student activities towards such mission could be seamlessly integrated with the existing curriculum so that the future members of the knowledge society are fully developed in all aspects of societal transformation. Thus, there are multiple technologies and appropriate management's structures that have to work together to generate a knowledge society."

WEALTH GENERATION

"The wealth generation is a very important task for the

nation, which has to be woven around national competencies. The task team has identified core areas that will spearhead our march towards knowledge society. The areas are: Information Technology, bio-technology, space technology, weather forecasting, disaster management, tele-medicine and tele-education, technologies to produce native knowledge products service sector and Infotainment which is the emerging area resulting from convergence of Information and entertainment. These core technologies, fortunately, can be interwoven by IT. The methodology of wealth generation in these core areas and to be able to meet an export target set at 50 billion dollars by the year 2008, especially using IT sector is subject of discussion while simultaneously developing capability to generate Information Technology products worth 30 billion dollars domestically to pump in for societal transformation. Evolution of policy and administrative procedures, changes in regulatory methods, identification of partners and most importantly creation of young and dynamic leaders are the components to be in place. In order to generate wealth, it is essential that simultaneously a citizen-centric approach to shaping of business policy, user-driven technology generation and intensified industry-lab-academia linkages have also to be established."

KNOWLEDGE INCREMENTALISM

While a knowledge society has a two-dimensional objective of societal transformation and wealth generation, a third dimension emerges if India is to transform itself into a knowledge superpower. This is knowledge protection and it entails a tremendous responsibility. Ancient India was a knowledge society that contributed a great deal to civilization. We need to recover that status and become a knowledge power. We must learn from our mistakes to achieve a better standard of life. A developed India will supplant a spirit of defeat with the spirit of victory. One of the important ingredients for a knowledge society is competitiveness that requires innovative systems, in turn demands consortium or cluster multiple institutions. The cluster consists of interdependent firms interactive on one side bridging institutions consisting of think tanks and technical constancy and the other side knowledge providing institutions like universities, colleges, R&D labs and technology providing firms. The dominant institutions of clusters are the actuators —users or the customers.

COMPETITIVENESS

The World Economic Forum has defined competitiveness as "the ability of national economy to achieve sustained high rates of economic growth". As per this definition ranking of different countries for 2002-03, according to the forum are: USA [1], Taiwan [3], Singapore [4], Australia [7], Hong Kong [17], China [33] and India [48]. "The world competitiveness is therefore decided by a triangular combination consisting of progressiveness of industry, technology push and status of governmental deregulation, all working in unison. Technology-led industrial growth can be sustained only through establishing an innovation system. It is through the process of innovation that knowledge is converted into wealth. Further, innovation is an important factor for the competitiveness of both service and manufacturing sectors and hence the urgent need to put in place an innovation system. Such a system would involve network of firms, knowledge-producing institutions, bridging institutions and customers/users in a value addition-creating production chain. With such a consortium, the innovation system would tap into the growing stock of global knowledge, assimilate and adapt it to local needs and finally create new knowledge and technology. India must evolve such systems to improve its competitiveness in a global marketplace. Competitiveness emerges from the strength of knowledge power, which is powered by technology that in turn is powered by capital. In the coming years, competitiveness would be derived from the ability to recognize and integrate all forms of knowledge leading to innovation in every area of human endeavor."

CHALLENGES

Dr. Kalam remarks: "The presence of a competitive environment, networking capabilities, wealth generation with social concern and above all ignited minds of the young: these are all very important ingredients for building a knowledge society. Whether a nation has arrived at a stage of knowledge society is judged by the way the country effectively deals with knowledge creation and development." In his analytical report in Business Line (November 25, 2003), G. Srinivasan has focused on the futuristic challenges in the Indian information super-highway. "For a country such as India, said to be cruising on the information super highway, with its innate strengths in software technology, and with a communication revolution in the making, it is hardly flattering for its technological prowess to be hit. But this is what happened, with the country ranged 119th, among 178 countries surveyed by the Geneva-based International Telecommunication Union (ITU), in the Digital Access Index (DAI)-combining eight variables, covering five areas such as the availability of infrastructure, affordability of access educational level, quality of ICT (information and communication technologies) services and Internet usage to provide an overall country score. Though India did not have much of a policy for the IT sector till recently when the sector became the cynosure of all for the laurels it had brought abroad, the Government did fashion a successful technology park paradigm. As the UNCTAD Report 2003 aptly appreciates, government policies in India to promote the IT services export industry include permitting duty-free imports of a spate of key IT products' allowing 100 percent foreign equity, deferring corporate income-tax until 2010, dedicated data communication links, single-window government clearance and providing single-point customs bonding and export certification. This was complemented by support to incubators, human resource training and the funding for venture capital. The report pertinently hastens to caution that "if ICT developments are limited to closed technology parks or zones and are not combined with other policies in the area of education and training, the gains will not diffuse throughout the economy. Hence, more attention needs to be paid to linking these strategies to the domestic industry and other related policies."

"India's Third Wave sector has been a spectacular success story. It has focused on outsource programming and date centre services. The range of functions and services needs to be widely broadened. So far India's success has been based on cheap labour and is, as such, inherently temporary... IT needs to expand into more advanced riches and also prepare for the fusion of IT and biology. India, will never be an economic giant till it puts aside the attitude that technological advance make life worse for the poor" (Alvin Toffler, *India Today*, March 17, 2003). In Dr. Kalam's new social order, 'connectivity' force is binding and invigorating societal transformation. It includes the integration of vital growth sectors, connectivity of rural-urban dynamics, networking of human and material resources and convergence of technologies.

2

Rural-Urban Divide: "Vision" Vignettes

S.P. GUPTA ET. AL.

"A Vision is not a project report or a plan target.

It is an articulation of the desired end results in broader terms."

—*A.P J Abdul Kalam*

VISION : A LIVING DYNAMIC REALITY

Our vision of India's future should be both comprehensive and harmonious. It must encompass all the myriad aspects that constitute the life of the country and its people. It must balance and synthesise all the divergent views and forces that compete in the pursuit of self-fulfilment. It must be based on an objective assessment of facts and a realistic appraisal of possibilities, yet it must rise beyond the limitations of past trends, immediate preoccupations and pressing challenges to perceive the emerging opportunities and concealed potentials.

Most of all, our vision of India's future should serve to awaken in all of us a greater awareness of our cultural and spiritual strengths—which formed the bedrock of our past achievements and should form the foundation of our future accomplishments. Some of our traditions must change, but knowledge, in essence is our greatest endowment. The vision should awaken in us an unswerving confidence in ourselves, a complete reliance on our own capacity as nation and an unshakable determination to realise our full potential. A true vision cannot be a static written statement. It must emerge as a living a dynamic reality in the minds and hearts of the people and their leaders.

TECHNOLOGY: A DECISIVE ROLE IN DEVELOPMENT

An essential requirement for envisioning India's future in the new century is to recognise that the parameters which determine national development have changed in recent years and will change future in future. This will open up greater possibilities than ever before. A powerful set of catalytic forces is accelerating the speed of social change throughout the world. They include a rapid rise in levels of education, high rates of technological innovation and application, ever faster and cheaper communication that dissolves physical and social barriers both within countries and internationally, greater availability and easier access to information, and the further opening up of global markets. These trends are representative of a relative shift in the engines that drive development from manufacturing to the services sector and from capital resources to human and knowledge resources. Technology, organisation, information, education and productive skills will therefore, play a critically decisive role in governing the future course of development.

URBAN DEVELOPMENT

Disparities between the social and physical infrastructure of the urban and rural areas are common to all countries. In India, they are a continuing source of concern and will become further aggravated unless innovative strategies are evolved to accelerate the development of rural infrastructure. A Vision of India 2020 must assess and try to anticipate the complexion of the future urban-rural divide.

Recent evidence confirms that the rate of growth of urban centres in the country is declining more rapidly that was previously anticipated, though the proportion of people living in urban areas continues to rise. According to the 2001 Census, 27.8 percent of the Indian population reside in cities, compared with 25.5 percent in 1990. The urban population is expected to rise to around 40 percent by 2020. As India's cities continue to swell, the challenge of improving the urban infrastructure will be magnified. For instance, only 73 percent of India's urban population has access to improved sanitation facilities, compared to the UMI reference level of 95 percent.

The trend towards concentration of urban population in a small number of large urban Centres has been taking shape over a century. While the number of urban centres double between 1901 and 1991, the urban population increased eight-fold, resulting in a top heavy urban hierarchy. Future demographic and economic growth is likely to concentrate in and around 60 to 70 large cities in the country having a population of a million people or more.

The demographic trends towards urbanisation are accompanied by a change in the management and financing of urban development as a result of liberalisation. Decentralisation of municipal governance has led to a substantial re-education in budgetary allocations for infrastructural development. Greater reliance is now placed on institutional financing and capital markets for resource mobilisation and on private companies for service delivery.

DISPARITIES IN URBAN INFRASTRUCTURE FACILITIES

Disparities in infrastructure between large and small urban areas have always been prevalent, but these disparities can be expected to increase significantly in future years. The stricter fiscal disciplines imposed by government and credit rating agencies will make it increasingly difficult for all but the largest urban centres to attract finance for infrastructural development. The large cities may be expected to experience modest to high rates of growth and to absorb a large part of the incremental migration in their peripheries and neighbouring towns. Being linked to the national and global economy, these large areas are likely to attract investment from the corporate sector and experience a stable demographic growth, while small and medium towns, particularly in backward regions, attract little industrial and infrastructural investment and report low and unstable demographic growth. This almost exclusive focus on improving infrastructure and basic amenities in the large cities is misplaced. Still greater inequality may be expected in the level of basic services across urban centres of different sizes by the year 2020, unless concerted initiative is taken to reverse the trend.

The gross inadequacies of infrastructure, specially those of public transport, water supply and sanitation, demand corrective action. A strategy for developing capabilities within the urban local bodies to cope with the infrastructural deficiencies must be adopted, with genuine decentralisation of financial and administrative powers and restructuring of the entities on the basis of sound management practices.

URBAN POVERTY

The face of urban poverty in 2020 is unlikely to be very different from what it is today, given that the largest indicator of poverty in cities is not so much lack of income, as lack of decent housing and civic amenities. These call for a change in a number of policies, especially those relating to land regulation, zoning, and development. The activities relating to provision of health care, water supply and sanitation, education and vocational training need to be carried out with higher levels of efficiency, to help the urban poor upgrade themselves.

While improving infrastructure in existing cities/towns is not to be ignored, in the next two decades there will be need to encourage growth of new townships and take up regional urban development plans where growth corridors can be identified and public-private partnerships promoted for investment in alternative nodes of development. Such centres will have considerable impact in improving the urban profile of the country. They will, however, need to make provision for adequate supply of water and sanitation as well as other civic amenities. They will also need to chalk out more liberal policies towards education and health care in order to attract a cosmopolitan group of investors, professionals and providers of other services. While a large part of it will cater to the affluent, through imaginative planning the new centres can serve the needs of the hinterland also by offering avenues for employment, housing and other needs of a large workforce.

Urban development represents one of the great challenges for India over the next two decades. Given the socio-political reality in India, it will be difficult for the private sector to bring about changes in the pattern of investment in infrastructure without the state becoming an active partner, bringing about the required legislative and administrative changes. A satisfying outcome will depend on the formulation of effective public policy to accelerate all-round development of smaller urban centres and to refashion the role of the state as an effective facilitator to compensate for the deficiencies of market mechanisms in the delivery of public goods. Anti-poverty programmers should primarily be directed towards creation of a community-based infrastructure.

RURAL INFRASTRUCTURE

Along with the development of urban infrastructure,

simultaneous efforts are also needed for strengthening rural infrastructure. Our vision is to create a rural infrastructure which connects every village with paved roads and telecommunication facilities, provides electricity and an assured supply of safe drinking water to all rural households, offers access to quality primary and secondary education to all children and medical services to all citizens.

The rural electrification programme, launched in 1951, has succeeded in bringing electricity to more than 5 lakh villages. However, 80,000 villages are yet to get electricity connections. Out of these, 18,000 are in remote areas where electrification through the conventional electricity grid may not be feasible. To achieve 100 percent rural energy specially for the remote villages.

But the problem of rural infrastructure cannot be viewed or tackled in terms of a composite of separate services or in isolation from changes affecting the urban landscape. A comprehensive and integrated strategy is required. The future development of urban centres will widen the disparities in civic infrastructure that exist between urban and rural communities, thereby stimulating greater migration to the cities and rapid expansion of urban slum areas. The natural growth of urban areas will make this trend inevitable unless bold steps are taken to promote an alternative, more geographically dispersed and equitable development paradigm. Past efforts to develop satellite townships and growth centres in the vicinity of large cities have mitigated the concentration of in the process it has furthered the concentration of population in mega cities.

ADVANTAGES OF RURAL LIVING

Rural living offer several considerable advantages over their urban counterparts. However, any successful alternative approach must address the crucial issues of infrastructure and civic amenities that make urban areas so attractive. One promising alternative is to link clusters of ten villages together by a high speed circular highway, thereby brining 100,000 or more people into a circular community that can be crossed within 30 minutes travel time, and promoting a balanced and well spread out development of urban services along the periphery of the ring road. This arrangement would vastly reduce the length and cost of constructing good roads between all the villages, enable establishment of quality services at any point around the ring to be accessible to all members of the linked community. Telecom links and sanitation system would naturally develop around the ring at far lower cost, and better quality schools and hospitals could develop to support the larger community. Industrial parks could be established to utilise the large workforce available within the ring. These and similar models need to be tried and modified, on a priority basis, otherwise it requires little stretch of imagination to anticipate the increasing congestion and immobility of large urban areas that is bound to occur in the near future.

ROAD CONNECTIVITY

A key component for rural development is the provision of roads for connectivity, access being essential for social and economic well-being. Families residing alongside roads benefit from better health and greater educational opportunities compared to the families living in remote villages. Based on current plans, all villages with more than 500 inhabitants will be connected by all-weather roads within the next decade.

Realisation of this vision will depend on many things, but most importantly on our self-confidence, self-reliance and determination to make it a reality. For that, we need first of all to abandon the sense of dependence and the urge to imitate other nations blindly. We need also to rediscover the well-springs of our own native strength, the rich endowments of our culture and spiritual tradition.—Report on "*India Vision 2020*" (2002).

[illegible] connectivity [illegible] within 50 [illegible] with [illegible] of the [illegible] establishment [illegible] separate [illegible] members [illegible] system [illegible] would develop [illegible] quality schools and hospitals [illegible] could be established [illegible] within [illegible] results. [illegible] of these rural areas that is found [illegible]

ROAD CONNECTIVITY

A key [illegible] is the [illegible] of rural [illegible] economic well-being [illegible] compared [illegible] current [illegible] within the next decade.

Realisation [illegible] but most importantly [illegible] determination to [illegible] reality [illegible] all to abandon the [illegible] dependence [illegible] unrealistic solutions [illegible] workings [illegible] of [illegible] 2020 (2002).

PART II

THE PURA REVOLUTION : CREATING "CONNECTIVITIES"

3

PURA: A Road Map for New Rural India

A.P.J. ABDUL KALAM

RURAL CONNECTIVITY

Over a period, a number of modern scientific and technological achievements have helped the rural areas as well. They have also affected rural life-styles, sometimes irreversibly. Modern fertilizer and agro-chemicals based high yield agriculture, health services, electricity, radio, television, bus services, agro-machinery and plastic footwear are a few examples. However, there has been an asymmetry between the rural and urban areas. Since urban areas are centres of industrial and business activities and also seats of political power, many facilities for better life are first established there. The economies of scale would also be cited as being influential in people taking such a decisions. Wealth begets wealth. Higher economic activity begets more economic activities and therefore more employment.

Therefore, migration from rural areas begins. Many underemployed persons move to the other cities in search of a better life. Per se this is not bad. But on the other hand, attention given to modern facilities in the rural areas is poor. A good doctor would not like to stay in the village, non would a good teacher. The asymmetry that is thus created takes a toll on the cities as well. Most cities are becoming unlivable as about 50 percent of their inhabitants live in slums or near slum conditions, or live so far away that they tire themselves in commuting. A number of studies have shown that beyond a size, it becomes much costlier to provide services to the increasing population in city than to establish a new city!

The new cities need not be brand new. Let us look at the nature of modern industries and the emerging scenario. The mass production of yesteryears is only confined to a few areas. It is possible to have a number of decentralized industries which maintain world-class levels and become part of a globally competitive industry. Electricity can be supplied anywhere. The vital modern telecommunication and IT infrastructure have made global connectivity instantaneous.

Therefore, it is possible to connect clusters of villages through a nearly annular ring of roads, with traffic designed in such a way that movement from one village to another can be quick and convenient. This help in many ways. Many agro-industries, services industries and even high-tech concerns, can be relocated in such villages by moving a few government offices and providing special concessions for industries. Once the process starts, economic activities will take care of the rest. These clusters have to be managed in an imaginative fashion, involving local people panchayats, business persons and the intelligentsia which will move in. The vision includes the building of many such clusters all over India. Some states have already shown interest in developing a few clusters.

India's economic growth still largely depends on agriculture. Modern technologies integrated with agriculture and agro-food industry will revolutions this sector and produce large scale employment and thereby wealth. It is said that "When users, implementers as well as knowledge and skill possessors are linked and networked, success comes effectively and in multiples". A network resource can impart a non-linear progressive addition to development and growth.

Nation in its development mode has to go through integrated development plan and empowered management structures in areas such as education, healthcare, agriculture and food processing, biotechnology, information and communication technology, strategic sectors, industries and building-up of infrastructure including power, networking of rivers and rural development through PURA.

RURAL DEVELOPMENT

India lives in villages, but because of the lack of proper education, employment, healthcare and infrastructure people migrate cities for a better living. The fact that there is net migration from villages to cities indicates that, in the opinion of the rural people, cities are better places to live or they get employment for sustaining their family. Ideally, both rural and urban areas should be equally attractive with no net migration either way. Near zero net rural-urban migration is a mark of completed development. How can we achieve that happy state of affairs? Rural connectivity is the only solution and the details are described as a process, which: (a) provides rural areas with all desirable amenities that are currently available only in cities; (b) will generate as a consequence employment on the same scale, and at the same level, as cities do; (c) will provide these benefits at a small fraction of the financial, social, cultural and ecological costs the cities have to bear. It is the expectation that this combination of employment and natural environment will make rural areas as attractive as cities are, if not even more attractive. Then, rural development may be expected to prevent, if not actually reverse, rural-urban migration. Presently, several technologies exist to make this possible provided we use multiple connectivity approach as brought out in Technology Vision 2020. Experience in India has demonstrated that the true handicap suffered by rural areas is poor connectivity and little else. That lacuna may be rectified by linking together a loop of villages by a ring road and high quality transport. That transport connectivity, creates in those linked villages a large enough market to support a variety of services, which the villages will not be able to do individually. Thereby, the loop road and the transport service together convert those villages immediately into a virtual town with a market of tens of thousands of people. Such a well-connected rural space (combined with state of the art telecommunication connectivity) will have a high probability of attaining rapid growth by setting up a virtuous circle – more connected people attracting more investment, and more investment attracting even more people and so on. Basically, this proposal involves: (a) selecting a ring of villages; (b) connecting the villages on the ring by establishing a high quality transport and telecommunication system; (c) encouraging reputed specialists to locate schools, hospitals and other social services around the ring; (d) marketing this well serviced space to attract industry and commerce; and (e) Internet connectivity. It can be seen that rural development is one of the important missions for transforming India into a developed nation as our country consists of 70 to 80% rural habitat. Apart from agriculture, road transportation, storage system, chilling plants, communication relating to multiple technology and management have to be networked. Involving Panchayati Raj Institutions in the State in implementing this programme is also a step in the right direction. I would, however, like to sound a note of caution and advice. It is customary for us city-dwellers to take for granted the rural people's requirements as we perceive them. Very often we give them what they do not want and we do not give them what they really want. It is essential that the requirements of the rural people are voiced by them and ascertained from them instead of prescribing them from above so that the money spent is not spent in vain. We are passing through times when constant dynamic changes in the environment are the order of the day. The whole world is literally galloping from one rung of the developmental ladder to another and any country failing to take steps to join the race, needless to say, will be sadly left behind.

PURA : A MULTIPLE-CONNECTIVITY APPROACH

I envisage Rural Models to share/augment service capabilities to cater to the IT enabled service demands from local in addition to foreign sources. Such models should aim to provide opportunity for rural economic development and prosperity we need connectivity among villages providing them urban amenities.

The PURA model envisages a habitat designed to improve the quality of life in rural areas and also makes special suggestions to remove urban congestion. Naturally, our most demanding urban problem is that of removal of congestion. Also, efficient supply of water and effective waste disposal in every locality are the paramount civic needs. There is a minimum size below which a habitat is not viable and not competitive within the existing congested city. At the same time, the existing congested city is not economical compared to a new town once the minimum size of expansion is crossed.

As against conventional city say, rectangular in shape and measuring 10 km, the model considers an annular ring-shaped town integrating minimum 10 to 15 villages of the same 60 km sq. area, and the same access distance of 1 km to transport arteries. It needs only one transportation route, half as long as that needed for the rectangular city; so the frequency of transportation will be doubled, halving waiting times. It has zero junctions and will need only a single-level layout. Also, it needs only one route as against eight needed for the rectangular plan, so people will no longer need for the rectangular plan, so people will no longer need to change from one line to another to move from any one point to another; that would save communicating time. Future, as all traffic is concentrated into one single route, high-efficiency mass transportation systems become economical, even for a comparatively small population. This cuts costs substantially and is more convenient for the general public.

Knowledge-power rural development is an essential need for transforming India into a knowledge superpower. High bandwidth rural connectivity is the minimum requirement to take education, healthcare, and economic dynamism to the rural areas. Providing Urban Amenities in Rural Areas (PURA) is essentially conceived around four types of connectivities, with the aim to speed up the process of achieving total rural prosperity.

PHYSICAL CONNECTIVITY

The first of these connectivities is Physical Connectivity movement of people and goods, access to schools, health centres and markets (Fig. 3.1). In our rural areas today, there are inadequate roads, rail and public infrastructure. With more than 580,000 villages in clusters, from 10 upwards.

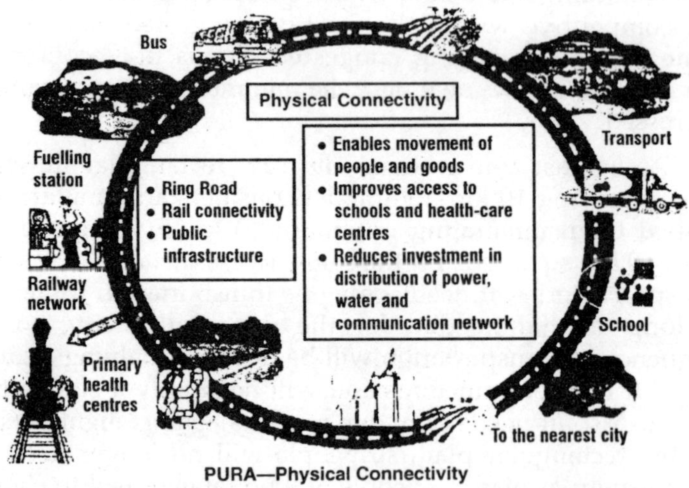

Fig. 3.1. PURA—Physical Connectivity

This cluster of villages needs to be provided physical connectivity by near ring roads. Low cost buses, preferably driven by batteries energised by renewable energy sources, and powered by high efficiency engine would be operated almost throughout the day as shuttle services moving people and goods from village to village and village to school, health centre, fuelling stations, farming areas, warehouses, agro-industries and other commercial centres.

Thus, the heart of the PURA concept is Physical Connectivity of 10 or more villages by a ring road covering a population of around 30,000–50,000 people. Connectivity, thereafter, to a rail network and to a nearest city beyond this village cluster would take off from the ring road. All these roads or links will be of high quality enabling high speed transportation.

This is potentially a cost effective solution for activating the schools, health centres, villages markets, warehouses and commercial centres that would serve the population of the entire cluster, thus resulting in economies of scale. Also these clusters will become an excellent investment destination because the transactional costs will be much lower than in the metropolis. In addition, quality of life will be improved.

ELECTRONIC CONNECTIVITY

Similarly, PURA needs to be provided with Electronic Connectivity (Fig. 3.2). The system-oriented approach for the village cluster would require to introduce tele-education for farmers and villagers, village internet kiosks, public call offices, tele-medicine, e-market, e-governance, e-commerce and so on. Thus, the revolution in Information Technology supported by space-based technology would create the needed societal transformation at the grass-roots of the country. It also will provide the opportunity for the villagers to collectively located call centres, business processing out souring and software development centres to use outside markets. Thus PURA provides a seamless connection and movement of molecules (people), atoms (material) and electrons (knowledge).

KNOWLEDGE CONNECTIVITY

Knowledge connectivity (Fig. 3.3) will transform the rural area with connectivity in education, healthcare, vocational

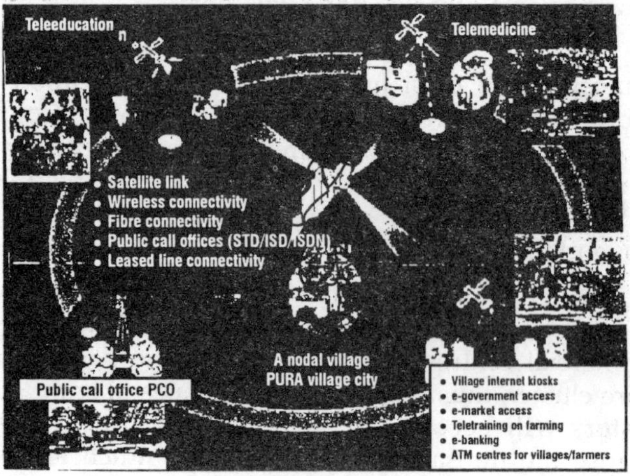

Fig. 3.2. PURA—Electronic Connectivity

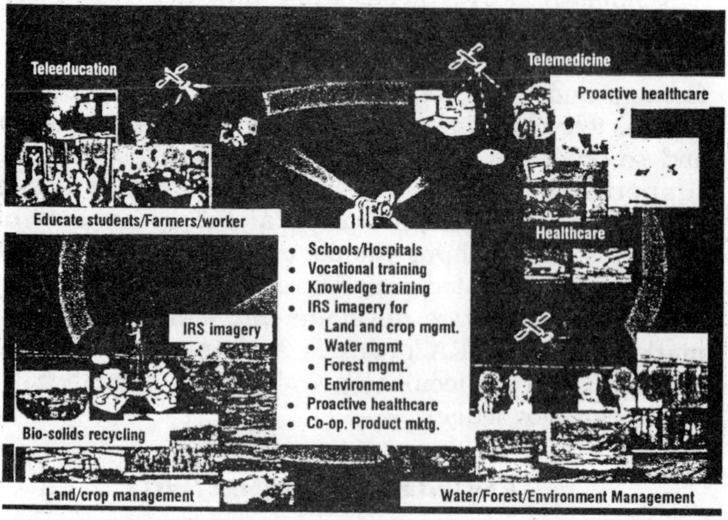

Fig. 3.3. PURA—Knowledge Connectivity

training, satellite application for crops water and forest management, environment protection and cooperative product marketing. The combination of electronic connectivity and knowledge connectivity will generate literacy movement, tele-education, healthcare and resource management.

ECONOMIC CONNECTIVITY

It would be seen therefore that the triad of physical, electronic and knowledge connectivity brings forth the economic connectivity (Fig. 3.4) through small-scale industries, agro and food processing, warehouses, micro power plants, renewable energy and village markets. This will generate larger employment opportunities, women empowerment and improved quality of life. The villages not only improve the quality of life but also maintain the rural beauty and environment. Moreover, the connectivities make the rural villages close to any part of the world.

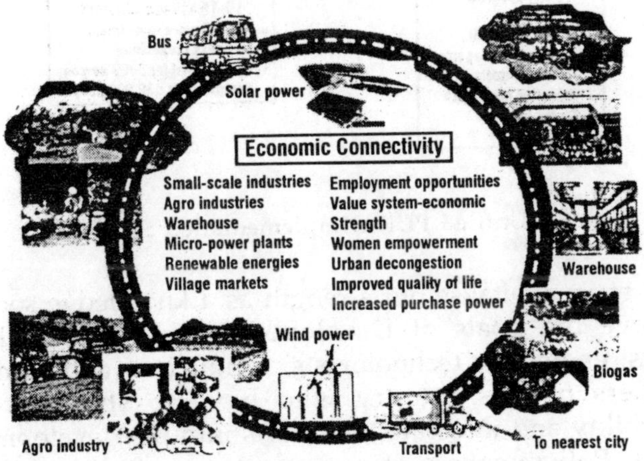

Fig. 3.4. PURA—Economic Connectivity

UNIFIED PURA IMPLEMENTATION STRATEGY

PURA has to be business proposition which is economically viable and managed by entrepreneurs and small-scale industrialists, as it involves education, health, power generation, transport and management. PURA needs an integrated development approach with empowered management structure. The integrated implementation strategy is brought out in Fig. 3.5.

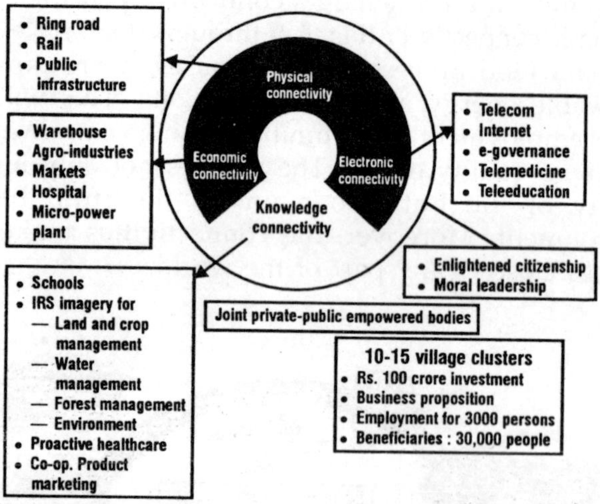

Fig. 3.5. Unified PURA Implementation Strategy

We must capitalise our strength as a knowledge society to achieve the goals of Developed India by 2020. It is scientists, engineers, technologists, technicians and farmers and others of this country who have to shoulder the responsibility and integrate the efforts into the development missions. Policy-makers of our country must help in this process of transforming the mission into actions. Challenges will always be there, but it is for us to convert them into opportunities for growth and development.—*Envisioning an Empowered Nation : Technology for Societal Transformation* (2004).

DR. KALAM'S SUGGESTIVE PURA PROGRAMMES

- "Youth in the rural localities could be easily trained to cater to requirement of IT enabled service industries. PURA will show how electronic connectivity can be used to reduce the load on physical transport network. For example, if you can find that you can book your railway tickets through the web in a secure and reliable way, you will not have to take the car or scooter and go to the railway station. Many day-to-day activities that require you to commute can be done electronically, even generating a new breed of workers—particularly in our Women—who telecommute."
- "Knowledge powered village complexes have to be generated in good numbers in every State. That means, 20–30 villages linked through a circular road (10x6 kms) with highways bringing physical connectivity. This knowledge powered village complex will also have markets attracting urban business. IT enabled service industries can flourish in rural complexes as we can get land and building at very lower rates. The best technology and processes in the world with right skilled and motivated people will have to be deployed to realize such mega projects."
- "In the periphery, there can be schools, primary health centres, crafts people working and training centres, silos for storage of products and markets for promoting products of craftspeople, cottage industries and Self Help Groups. This knowledge powered village complex will also have markets attracting urban business."
- "I would urge the leading industrialists of the State and also the representative of the apex industry organization . . . to consider adopting a group of villages, in partnership with banks and financial institutions, for providing urban facilities to them.

These rural complexes should be economically self-sustaining and form the backbone of developed Bihar".

SUGGESTED ROLE OF VILLAGERS IN PURA

The village leaders can create awareness about PURA amongst the village community so that they can come forward to willingly contribute in this development programme. The contribution could be in the form of: (a) Promoting and facilitating illiteracy eradication campaigns in the village. (b) Explaining the usefulness of computer education in village administration for providing transparent governance and economic advancement. (c) Forming village cooperatives for central procurement, storage, preservation, processing and marketing the goods at attractive price. (d) Working for providing better nutrition, sanitation facilities, safe drinking water and access to reproductive healthcare for healthy families and communities. (e) Fighting against the social evils such as dowry, female foeticide, child marriage, child labour, domestic violence, and ill-treatment and harassment of the socially backward classes. (f) Encouraging women to attain independence through formation of Self Help Groups with the help of micro-credit and organising various skill training programmes. (g) Facilitating the conservation of energy through effective utilization of solar power, recycling the waste for energy generation and management of water through rainwater harvesting, etc.

- "The Universities can take this as theatre of action. Out of 6 lakh villages in the country, about 50,000 PURA complexes would emerge. What is the type of farming to be chosen, area under cultivation, water management, production, food processing and marketing is a task of paramount effort. The Universities can consider the PURA model to be implemented in various regions keeping the following variables in mind:

A. Number of villages per complex;

B. Number of village-complexes for the state;

C. Crop pattern for different complexes based on soil, weather, core competence, water availability and region (hill or plain);

D. Cultivation methods;

E. Food processing units; and

F. Marketing centres.

The model should enable proper selection of clusters and deployment of our youth in different areas of agriculture, agro-processing and the market to make this programme a reality.

- "Each PURA should have a separate handicraft co-operative society which will ensure timely supply of sustainable raw material, industrialists and entrepreneurs can establish handicrafts and handloom production units using the core competence of the region. I find that so far the nation has awarded 763 master craft persons and weavers during the last four decades. I would suggest we can make use of their talent in shaping the industry by asking them to be facilitators in their areas of specialization in respective regions. They can provide innovative ideas on product design, guidance and suggestions on improving the productivity, conduct training and vocational education for the younger generation and also give ideas on alternative products. In some cases they can also be funded to become entrepreneurs with suitable entrepreneurship training. These master craft persons should be supported by the entrepreneurs by providing them all the infrastructural support and marketing support."

- "PURA has to be a business proposition economically viable and managed by entrepreneurs and small scale industrialists, as it involves education, health, power generation, transport and management. Government's support should be available in empowering such management agencies in providing initially economic support and finding the right types of management structure and the leaders to manage. The PURA scheme makes clusters of villages developed, in addition to maintaining rural beauty."

— Compiled from the *President's Speeches*

PURA AND POLICY INITIATIVES

PURA scheme is to be implemented in 5000 rural clusters across the country in the next five years.

—**Mr. A.B. Vajpayee,** Prime Minister, in his *Independence Day Address,* August 15, 2003

PURA (Provision of Urban Amenities in Rural Areas) scheme in 10,000 rural clusters to be launched before August 15, and village electrification to be completed by 2007 to cover one-crore households and one lakh villages.

—National Democratic Alliance (NDA), *Election Manifesto,* April 8, 2004

A substantial portion of Government's investment will be channelised to the villages, with special emphasis on improving basis infrastructure such as roads, power and drinking water in rural areas. Connectivity of village complexes for providing economic opportunities to all segments of people will get special emphasis to bridge the rural-urban divide.

—**Dr. A.P.J. Abdul Kalam,** *Address to Parliament,* June 7, 2004

New Deal for Rural India: "This new deal must encompass investment in irrigation, credit delivery, availability of electricity, primary education, rural roads and modernization of farm sector infrastructure."

—**Dr. Manmohan Singh,** Prime Minister, in his *Independence Day Address,* August 15, 2004

Boosting agricultural growth through diversification and development of agro-processing is one of the objectives of the National Common Minimum Programme (NCMP). The Prime Minister in his address to the Nation on June 24, 2004 promised a "New Deal" for rural India. This new deal is not only essential for rural development and welfare, but also essential for achieving sustained overall annual growth of 7-8% and generating employment.

—**Mr. P. Chidambaram,** Finance Minister in his *Budget for 2004-05,* July 8, 2004

A beginning has also been made for a new scheme such as the Provision of Urban Amenities in Rural Areas for water harvesting and restoration of water tables, upgradation of 100 ITIs.

—**Dr. Montek Singh Ahluwalia,** Deputy Chairman, Planning Commission in his *Press Briefing,* September 9, 2004

4

PURA: Challenges and Opportunities

P.V. INDIRESAN

I
DEVELOPMENTAL DIMENSIONS

Dr. Kalam's vision is to make India a development country in another 15-20 years. That raises the question, "What makes a nation a development one?." There is a fable of a pious person who prayed to God for long years until finally God agreed to grant him a boon, but one boon only. The old man thought about it shrewdly, and then asked of God: I want to feed milk to my grand son's grandson in a golden cup while standing on top of the seven story family mansion enjoying the beauty of its garden. The boon he asked was one only but it had many dimensions including long life, good health, progeny for several generations, wealth, good environment and the like we could drum up a similar situation for our own vision of development.

These days the state of development is measured by the Human Development Index, a measure fine-tuned by the UNDP. That has three components : Per capita income, educational attainment, and life expectancy. Dr. Chidambaram, Dr. Kalam's successor at TIFAC, has worked out that these three could be collapsed into two: Female literacy and per capita electricity consumption. That implies that once female literacy and electricity consumption are increased, virtually everything else will fall in place, and development will follow automatically.

Kalam's Development Path

Out of a score reports from TIFAC Vision 2020 exercises, Dr. Abdul Kalam has chosen six: Value-addition in agriculture, education, health, connectivity, strategic industries and composite rural development according to plan PURA, as the thrust areas for making India a developed nation. One may question the choices he has made but there can be no doubt that his vision comes as fresh breeze of a win-win game in our murky political on a win-lose basis.

PURA: A Strip of Habitation

PURA is a strip of habitation about 500 meters wide on either side of a ring road linking a loop of villages. Hence, every point in PURA will be within walking distance from open farms on one side and a modern road transport system on the other. Places of work will normally be within walking distance. It will have broad uncrowned streets; gracious pathways. PURA will restore the joy of walking. Dr. Kalam has talked about PURA day in and day out. At long last he has made a convert of even the Prime Minister who in his Independence Day speech, promised to establish 5,000 of them. In that case, virtually every village will be within 5 km of one ring will offer so much dwelling space that no family need suffer from lack of shelter. Slums in cities, and huts in villages, will disappear. Thus, the dream of PURA is.

- From slums or huts to garden house.
- From congested streets to gracious paths.
- From manual labour to knowledge occupation.

Many hard-headed businesspersons have similar dreams. They are donating large sums as charity for rural development. However generous they may be, charity will always come in driblets. On the other hand, if PURA were to become a commercially profitable proposition, the sky will be the limit. Then only will PURA become a reality, and not remain a dream.

Uniqueness of PURA

PURA differs from the conventional ideas of economic development of rural areas in six different ways:

(a) It aims at a comprehensive development of rural areas to generate urban-level incomes, and not mere "poverty alleviation".

(b) It plans for an investment at urban levels and not the much lower amounts that prevails at present.

(c) It aims to generate employment for the educated, thereby, halt and even reverse rural-urban migration.

(d) It treats quality infrastructure as the prerequisite and not the consequence of development.

(e) It seeks modern industry, investment in social and commercial service instead of rural handicrafts and agri-based small industry.

(f) It relies on private initiative. It is a for-profit enterprise not dependent on subsidy from the government.

Conventional rural development schemes suffer from two basic flaws: Jobs that are created pay subsistence wages only and not the substantial salaries the organised sector pays. Two, the products are aimed at the local market, which is neither large nor assured. PURA removes these road blocks by starting with an entrepreneur who brings in an assured global market and creates jobs that pay the substantial wages of the organised sector. However, this kind of exercise needs expert staff who will insist on getting a choice of schools, nursing homes, shopping malls, recreation facilities, and of course, physical, electronic, economic and knowledge connectivity. A minimum size of population for a habitat to offer an acceptable bouquet of services.

India has, currently, 28.1 million employees in the organised sector, of whom 9 million are in productive activities, and the remaining in various services. Almost all these jobs are located in the remaining in various services. Almost all these jobs are located in the urban areas where the population is about 300 million. Hence, as a thumb rule, we may take it that number of jobs in the services. Then for a minimum population size of 30,000 PURA needs an infusion of at least 1,000 jobs in organised production, plus creation of another two thousand to meet consequential demands in the services sector.

Cost Advantages

PURA's unusual physical design in the form of a ring offers many cost advantages: Compared to conventional town plans, all infrastructure lengths are halved. Workplace and residence can be co-located to avoid daily commuting. Local water harvesting, water recycling and waste disposal become feasible. Hence, unlike in cities, these services will not have to bear large transportation costs. Located as they are in a rural area, real-estate prices will naturally be a fraction of what they are in cities. In addition, PURA offers a high quality habitat. With these advantages, PURA can be expected to grow rapidly once it receives the following three types of artificial insemination:

- Export businesses employing in all around a thousand, many of whom will be brought from outside to sow the seed of reverse rural-urban migration.
- A ring road about 30-40 km in length and connecting

at least 30,000 people with fast and frequent public transport.

- A parallel establishment of a wide range of consumer services.

Rural Ambience

Rural ambience has two unique characteristics. It is inward looking; villagers have intimate human contact with their neighbours, even with employers. They share each others' joys and sorrows. If they work under an employer, those employers too live in the same environment as the workers do. However bad the employers, there is human contact between employer and employee every day. In cities, organisations tend to be large; most employees do not even know who their employers are. The work atmosphere is mechanical, dehumanised. In consequence, neighbours do not have much to share among themselves, least of all, work experiences.

Above all, the most striking contrast between villages and cities arises in connection with the manner of reaching the place of work. In villages workers usually walk to work. A few many take a cycle. Even the rich who may have motorised vehicles use them for occasional business or for social purposes and not for daily commuting. In cities, almost without exception, everyone commutes over long distances and for long periods of time, at times, as much as two hours each way. Commuting imposes the most extensive and pernicious costs on cities. It costs money, as much a lakhs of rupees per employee to run buses and trains, and to build flyovers and metros. Commuting wastes time too. Typically, in metros, commuters spend two years or more of their lives in travelling to work, and do so under trying conditions. That hurts their psychology to the extent commuters tend to become self-centred, more interested in themselves than in others. It diminishes social cohesiveness with long hours spent away at work and in commuting, destroying family togetherness. Even the culture is affected; urban dwellers are less interested in the richness of tradition, in spirituality.

Neither is the existing rural ambience perfect. Cities offer privacy; villages do not. Villagers may know their employers but employers could be inhuman without any opportunity for redress. Cities offer high wages, a variety of job opportunities that cater to every taste and capability. Village jobs pay little, and offer little scope for varied talents. Village life can be stultifying, not rich and varied a city lights are. That is why rural ambience is not enough; we need urban amenities too.

Cities offer wide-ranging job opportunities with such a large variety that virtually every kind of talent finds scope. The numbers too are so large that both husbands and wives can be confident of securing satisfactory employment. Cities offer also better residences, piped, protected water supply, as well as more stable electricity. Then, a Vision that meshes urban amenities with rural ambience can be described in terms of a habitat where even the poorest live in modern residences fitted with piped water, modern sanitation, smokeless fuel, and reliable electric supply. There is no technical problem in providing these amenities in villages as well as they are in cities. In fact, the costs will be much less. While urbanisation is not needed at all for assuring any of these amenities, jobs and markets are a different matter altogether. Both of them need large catchment populations – the larger the better.

Urban Amenities and Rural Ambience

The problem of combining urban amenities with rural ambience boils down to the question of linking together large populations without the need to commute long distances each day to work, and to inducing neighbours to share their joys and sorrows together. The solution to both minimising daily commuting on the one hand and promoting neighbourliness on the other is simple and the same for both: Make it a rule that every employers gets space both for work and employee residences in one lot, within walking distance of each other. This solution is not unusual. Many institutions including the IITs, laboratories of the DRDO, Space, CSIR and atomic energy establishments as well as many agriculture-based industries have workplace and residence close together. Those campuses attract highly qualified experts offering amenities as good as any in the world. For the reason all residents are linked to the same employer, they share many joys and sorrows together. Though sophisticated, those campuses are essentially villages. They inculcate the kind of neighbourliness that is the hallmark of rural ambience.

Rural ambience means also that green fields should be within sight. For that reasons, PURA is confined to a strip no farther then 500 metres of the road that strings the campuses. That will guarantee that residences will be within walking distance, not more than 500 metres, from open fields on one side, and a highway on the other. That is why PURA is devised as a collection of village-sized campuses, each one enjoying all four connectivities that President Kalam advocates. They are stringed together in the form of a garland with a ring road as the string. Every point will then be urban because it will be within walking distance of the ring road that connects a city-size population. It is also rural because each is a campus where people have common interests. Further, they are also within walking distance of ring road that connects a city-size population. It is also rural because each is a campus where people have common interests. Further, they are also within walking distance of wide, open fields.

Role of Rurbanisers

Rural transformation is a complex process requiring the cooperation of promoters, service providers (both state and private), town planners, the construction industry, officials of several ministries, and most important of all the local population. Someone has to coordinate their activities, resolve mutual conflicts, and make them cooperate with one another. Usually, the government takes on this responsibility, but has not met with much success so far. Hence, Dr. Kalam has been seeking the help of some religious leaders who have been actively supporting development projects. Jawaharalal Nehru passionately opposed religiosity in any form, and his policy still rules. For a change, Dr. Kalam is trying to interest such agencies as the Mata Amritanandamayi Foundation to act as unifiers. It is possible that Nehru made a mistake. Instead of condemning religious fervor, it may be wiser to divert it to productive channels. In theory, reserving as little as 5 percent of the total area of a habitat to the poor should suffice to prevent slums. However, such a simple rule cannot be applied inside a city, and not even inside our villages that are no less congested than cities are. That is the reason why, PURA is planned for the space on either side of a ring road, a road that is away from cities, and bypassed villages too. Being neither rural nor urban, PURA needs a new breed of town planners, whom we may describe as Rurbanisers.

We are expert at starting new activities but poor in maintaining them. Management guru Prof. C.K. Prahalad once remarked that he was happy working in IIM Ahmedabad but had to quit because he could not get a gas connection even in that large city. This absence of such basic amenities as reliable electricity and safe drinking water is known as the *bijli, paani* problem. Rural transformation will not sustainable until these problems are resolved, and basic services are raised to international standards. Maintenance of such standards requires a new type of quality control, a new breed of auditors. These auditors will audit performance rather than expenditure. In particular, they will check that no impediments to future growth are created either inadvertently or deliberately. A Rurban habitat will lose its value if it grows into a traditional Indian *bazaar*. Checking that such bottlenecks do not develop will be a major responsibility of this new breed of auditors. They will also check on social, environmental, and psychological strains.

Financial Implications

PURA is a scheme to enhance physical, knowledge, economic, societal and electronic connectivities, of the rural areas starting with the construction of ring roads to link a loop of villages. It is to the credit of Dr. Kalam's persistence, and to his persuasive powers, that the Union Cabinet has now approved a proposal for implementing PURA, not as an experiment but nationwide. The scheme approved by the Cabinet envisages development of over 4,000 rural clusters located in backward areas. A sum of Rs. 3 crore has been allotted per cluster; over Rs. 12,000 crore in all. That is a huge sum, but from another perspective, it is not large at all. The Tenth Plan envisages an investment of about Rs. 20,000 per capita. Typically, rural development blocks have a population of about 1,00,000. Then, on a per capita basis, each block should get an investment of Rs. 200 crore, nothing less. Not all that investment will be from the Central or State governments; mainly, it will come from the private sector. Even then, the proposed expenditure of Rs. 3 crore is minuscule compared to what urban areas of same size population enjoy.

To Kalam, "PURA is one of the mechanisms which will be utilised for transforming our villages into a productive economic zone. Each PURA might call for an average investment of Rs. 100 crore (or about $ 20 million)."

Implementational Challenges

We can now visualize the manner in which PURA may be implemented:

- A promoter (or a consortium of promoters) initiates the process by offering to establish in a rural area an export business employing around a thousand workers.
- A respected foundation comes forward to act as the Unifier. It finalises an economical alignment of a ring road to link a set of villages.
- Assured of financial investment from the promoters, and organisational support from a respected NGO, the government makes a commitment to acquire land for the ring road, enough to expand into an expressway. It will also agree to construct the road, and zone the space on either side to form a quality Rurban habitat.

- With assurances from both promoters and the Government, the Unifier markets the space on either side of the ring road and puts together a consortium to provide a wide range of urban services including training of local populace for the new jobs that will emerge.
- Once the financial closure is complete for all these activities, and only then, the project is initiated.
- Independent Auditors are appointed to assure that global infrastructure standards are maintained, and no roadblocks are created to impede rapid, healthy growth.

Modalities

In confining the PURA scheme to strictly backward areas, the Government has evidently been motivated by political and humanitarian concerns. Such areas are too poor to make any contribution, or manage on their own. Hence, the Government had no option but to make PURA a grant-in-aid scheme to be administered by the District Collector. Unfortunately, district collectors are already overburdened by hundreds of other chores; they cannot pay the amount of attention PURA needs. District Collectors are also liable to be transferred at short notice, and hence, continuity is likely to be a frequent casualty. Just as it is desirable to bridge the gap between backward rural areas and relatively developed ones, it is equally desirable to bridge the gap between cities and the not-so-backward villages in their vicinity. In the latter case, PURA should aim to restrain rural-urban migration by maximizing educated employment. That will help cities too by decongesting them and removing the slums. Creating jobs for educated youth is expensive. Investments will have to be comparable to urban ones, around Rs. 100 crore or more per rural block. Then, grant-in-aid schemes will not suffice; private investment will be critical. Such an advanced PURA can be sustained only as a bankable, profit making business venture. It will usefully complement the barebones scheme that the Planning Commission has initiated, and help those villages that have been left out.

Connectivity Dynamics

Connectivity of PURA is its driving force, and organized sector employment is the primary force multiplier. The goods and services high-wage employees consume create a secondary force multiplier that will multiply the employment created by the initial investment. That is, villages are transformed in two steps: One, organized business creates high-wage educated employment by producing goods and services for sale outside PURA; two, the local goods and services high-wage employees consume multiplies such employment locally. With both steps in place, PURA is expected to become commercially profitable, self-supporting and as regenerative as cities are. This, form of PURA is export-oriented whereas conventional methods of rural development mostly aim at import-substitution. Thus, this advanced PURA will enjoy all the benefits that export trade confers. This modified scheme casts least burden on the cash-strapped State and Central government, and gives maximum scope for private initiative. In particular, the State government's responsibility is confined to help in acquiring enough land for development and in zoning it. It would be nice if State governments minimize also the obstructionism of their procedures. However, one stipulation is crucial. Businesses should organize housing for all their employees, and get them to reside inside PURA and not let them to commute from outside.

Spread Effect

The resultant political pressure should ensure the PURA spreads in stead of getting more and more concentrated at one point. Such a spread effect does not happen in the case of urban development because cities are isolated entities, and accepted as materially different from villages. Hence, not much political pressure develops when cities grow at the expense of villages—that is accepted as fate! However, it will not be the same fatalistic acceptance when one Rural

Development Block expands, and others in the neighborhood do not get the same chance to develop. However, all these virtuous circles can take hold only when it is realised that PURA is very different from conventional development schemes, where different agencies can survive and prosper too even when acting in isolation. In PURA, the first letter 'P' stands for participation. Several agencies that may otherwise compete bitterly will have to participate and cooperate. That is particularly true at the Centre where partitions between ministries are very rigid and sacrosanct.

As PURA stands, involving four different connectivities and further private development too it cannot be any particular department's baby, and hence like to remain an orphan as no department's baby. Hence, it is necessary to launch PURA as an independent mission the same way space programmers and atomic energy projects were. As in their case, it would be useful if the PURA mission comes directly under the Prime Minister. In essence, the objective of PURA is to reverse rural-urban migration. Hence, it has two dimensions to it: One, make the rural areas absolutely attractive to educated youth who are the most likely to migrate, and two, make cities unattractive, and repel the thought of further immigration.

Congestion Taxes

PURA makes rural ambience more attractive. It is best that, simultaneously, additional costs are imposed on cities too, and make them less attractive. An additional charge on cities is advocated not on account of bias but on sound economic grounds. Cities suck national resources excessively, and offer insufficient benefits in return. Flyovers and metros are not a good in themselves but a remedy for the illness of the city being overweight. More specifically, the Finance Ministry should consider seriously the imposition of Congestion Taxes on cities both as a deterrent against over-expansion, and as a source of new revenue to fund PURA. Three types of Congestion Taxes are in order: A tax on high priced real-estate; a tax on encroachment on public space, and the third on entry of vehicle to congested cities. In all our cities, real-estate prices bear no relation to the actual cost of construction. The benefits of such high prices are captured by speculators, and government benefits little from such speculations. Those high prices lead to crime, and have even funded terrorists.

Several cities have already introduced self-assessment schemes that have brought real-estate taxes to more reasonable levels. That is not enough. Taxes should be linked to: (a) Floor Space Ratio of each building, and (b) privately occupied space to the total in each neighbourhood. The former will deter the construction of high-rise apartments, and the latter over-exploitation of space leaving little for public use such as roads, gardens and playgrounds. Each way the environment will improve. Encroachment of public space has reached alarming levels. In all fairness, those who occupy valuable public space (often with market values of several lakh rupees) should pay for the benefit they get, and for the inconvenience they cause. It is fundamental principle of urban expansion that as cities grow, they shed industries, and concentrate on services. It is best to locate industries in the rural areas, and in small towns both for minimising the risk of catastrophe. For instance, if only the Union Carbide plant had been in a rural area the Bhopal disaster would not have been the catastrophe it became. A tax on excessive power consumption and on the entry of goods vehicles will divert industries from cities to more benign areas.

II
A GREAT STEP TOWARDS PURA

PURA and HUDCO

The Scheme PURA (Providing Urban-amenities in Rural Areas) has crossed an important hurdle: Dr. P.S. Rana, CMD of HUDCO, has offered to finance, on an experimental basis, the start-up costs of establishing PURA in a few viable locations. HUDCO's offer provides a chance to try out PURA as a for-profit, self-financing commercial project. The capital for this PURA scheme will be in three parts: (a) usual grants of the Central Government for rural development, (b) venture capital from HUDCO, and (c) normal business investment to meet expected increases in market demand. Hopefully, government grants for rural development will be available to HUDCO as seed capital. The venture capital contributed by HUDCO will be several times larger, large enough to install urban quality infrastructure rather that the much lower quality that villages are allowed to have at present. At a second level of hope, private ventures would be attracted by this superior infrastructure .

Rural Investment—Employment Multiplier

This model of PURA amplifies the funds that the Centre provides for rural investment in two stages. One, HUDCO raises three four times what the Central Government provides. Two, private investors multiply 3-4 times what the Centre and HUDCO jointly investment. Taken together, the final investment increases by a factor of ten or more. That enables an entirely new paradigm of rural development to be put into operation. Traditionally, across the political spectrum, most policy-makers in India have treated poverty alleviation as the primary objective of rural development. Invariably, towards that end, they give outright grants to villages-level functionaries. Due to budget constraints, such grants are usually sub-optimal, and, to make matters worse, middlemen siphon off the most part. Hence, the exercise is often infructuous: Roads do not last even one monsoon; hospitals have no medicines; teachers abscond. PURA corrects that wastage sources above the minimum threshold for sustainability. In addition, due to political pressures, government grants cannot be terminated however inefficient or vitiated by corruption they may be. Private investments have no choice but stay efficient: The moment they cease to be productive, the flow of money will dry up. Hence, unlike government grants, private investments self-terminate the moment they become ineffective.

In place of doles, PURA tackles rural poverty by generating wage employment. It even hopes to reverse rural-urban migration by attracting high-end jobs that are currently the monopoly of large cities. For that reason PURA will be located near fast expanding cities. That is not as idealistic as going to the most backward of the backward districts but it stands a better chance of success. As villages near cities are more populous, it will still address a large proportion of the rural population.

Venture Capital and Transport Connectivity

HUDCO has offered to provide venture capital to: (a) construct a ring road to link a loop of villages, as also a link road to connect that ring road to a highway emanating from the city; (b) run bus services on the ring road; and (c) develop a modern habitat on either side of the ring road to a width of 200-500 metres. The quality of transport will be as good as, or even better than, in cities. With these inputs, a population of nearly 50,000 will be connected immediately with scope for substantial expansion. With so many people connected together, the market becomes large enough to support a variety of services that no village can sustain buy itself. That provides a double benefit: One, new ventures will emerge, from restaurants and vehicle repair shops to English medium schools and cinema theatres, creating new jobs, including many for educated youth. Two, those jobs will check rural-urban migration improving Quality of Life in both villages and in cities.

However, there is a catch: As rural development specialists point out, in theory, rural roads can attract new jobs but, in practice, they rarely do. That happens because quality transport helps on the supply side only by making it cheaper to set-up new production units. However, on the demand side, it cannot create by itself additional purchasing power. As transport connectivity removes only the supple side bottleneck and not the bottleneck on the demand side, it is a necessary but not a sufficient condition for rural development. That explains why officials of the Urban Development Ministry have been optimistic about PURA a cheaper way of creating urban amenities. The latter have seen many promising rural development schemes fail; they are cautious if not skeptical.

Big Push for Export Business

To appreciate how the demand side bottleneck develops, let us consider what happens when incomes rise. By Engel's Law, when incomes rise, the demand increases sharply for such non-basic goods as radios and cycles, and even for luxury items like TV sets and cars. As a rule, all these goods will have to be imported from outside the rural development area, and to match that increase in imports, the rural area should increase its exports. Conversely, in the absence of exports no matter what schemes one may devise, villagers cannot import the goods bought by the rich; they cannot get rich. It is an Iron Law that the higher the per capita export income, the higher the capacity to import, and greater the purchasing power. The operative parameter here is "per capita" export income.

Hence, exports should be of products with high labour productivity. Interestingly enough, that productivity condition need not apply for goods of local consumption: A restaurant may have many waiters; schools may have small sizes. Such locally produced goods and services increase employment but do not hurt purchasing power. Only in the case of production for export it is important to have high value-addition high labour productivity.

Unfortunately, this fact is not common knowledge. Therefore, rural development schemes concentrate on capital-saving, labour-intensive production only; they do not allow for capital-intensive production, which is essential for high value exports. Handlooms, handicrafts, micro-finance and such other low cost additions to the rural economy can make marginal improvements only. They cannot make villages rich however good the connectivity may be. If villages can become rich only through capital-intensive production, then they should attract large producers also. Such producers pay highly wages. In sympathy, wages in local services too will increase. Thus, real purchasing power will increase all round, up to a level exports match the rise in the demand for imported goods. In other words, quality infrastructure is an enabler not a guarantor of rural prosperity; village can celebrate only when they attract large export businesses. A seed of a least 500 high-value jobs in the export sector will be needed before a PURA can take off. Thus, with HUDCO's offer of venture capital for physical infrastructure, PURA crosses one hurdle only. It faces yet another hurdle-at-tracing export businesses.

Four-Step Interdependent Process

Actually, PURA is a four-step process with four hurdles to cross: One, the State government should be supportive: It should agree to acquire land for the ring road, it should enforce zoning regulation to make the space on either side an attractive habitat. I should also agree to hand over the implementation of PURA to a commercial corporation. Fortunately, in CIDCO, which has been developing Navi Mumbai with great success, there is an attractive precedent. Two, with the assured patronage of the State government, a venture capitalist like HUDCO should come forward to supplement the meagre finances the Centre can provide. Three, after both the government and the venture capitalist commit to implement PURA, villagers should agree to part with their land on reasonable terms. Finally, at the fourth stage, modern export businesses should agree to join. HUDCO's offer means that of these four hurdles, only one has been crossed and three more still remain. For the skeptic, that means the door is three-fourths closed; for the optimist, it is one-fourth open. For the visionary that is enough: even the longest journey starts with but one step.

III
PUBLIC-PRIVATE PARTNERSHIPS

Corporate Social Responsibility

These days, it is fashionable to talk of Corporate Social Responsibility (CSR). It is commonly understood that CSR is the same as corporate charity. If that were so, CSR will only throw a few crumbs around; it will never take-off. For CSR to truly succeed, it should become an integral part of the corporation's profit-seeking process. That will happen if CSR is designed to increase the prosperity of the citizens at large. That CSR will be twice blessed: It blesseth the citizen with increased purchasing power; it blesseth the corporation with a larger market. Because the purchasing power of money is higher in villages that in expensive cities, it will be in the self-interest of large producers to shift their production to the rural areas. In the absence of reliable transport, that is not feasible at present. PURA corrects that defect. PURA offers a profitable opportunity for businesses to implement CSR merely by shifting to rural areas, it helps large businesses to satisfy both mammon and God simultaneously.

Major Impediments

There are three major impediments to be overcome. One, businessmen are hard-headed, and will not invest in the rural areas in the hope of long-term benefits; they like to see immediate profit. Two, farmers often get greedy; they demand execessive compensation for the land they surrender, and thereby destroy the only USP they have. Three, the basic problem of rural poverty is not that of inadequate supply, but one of poor demand. It is not difficult to organize production in rural areas, but villagers are too poor to buy what can be produced in villages.

Private investment will come only where local farmers are hospitable, and not where their demands are execessive. Such excesses can be restricted by forcing farmers to compete among themselves to get a PURA. Towards that end, several possibilities for the ring road may first be identified, and PURA located wherever the farmers offer the most economical package. Then, there will be little incentive for farmers to hike up prices. However, farmers should be guaranteed inflation – protected return substantially higher than what they earn at present; they should, on no account, be exploited.

Induced Private Investment

Inducing businesses to invest in rural areas, even in those that are close to cities, is a tough challenge. The following steps may be tried for that purpose: An autonomous corporation, which we may describe as Rurbaniser, having equity from government, local administration and private enterprise, identifies a selection of ring road alignments in the vicinity of an expanding city and propose the same to local farmers with a proposal that they offer their land for development on long lease of, say, 99 years. (Getting land on lease instead of by purchase minimizes initial capital outlay and risk too.) After identifying the best offer received from the farmers, Rurbanisers secure the support of the state government to build the ring road (with scope for future widening) using central funds. The State government's help is also sought for zoning the space on either side of the ring road, and for the simplification of real estate transactions. Once support from local farmers and the state government is assured. the Rurbaniser approaches venture capitalists to underwrite the interest costs of connectivity for the gestation period (around three years). With funds for connectivity in place, the Rurbaniser holds a road show for prospective employers in the organized sector inviting them to shift any expansion of their business from the crowded city to PURA in return for lower prices and superior environment. However, employers should agree to house their employees inside PURA.

Banks help by offering low-cost credit: (a) to venture capitalists for developing connectivity, (b) to employers for starting their business, and (c) to employees to construct their houses. The Centre minimizes investment risk by sharing interest costs during the gestation period. This modified PURA will be a useful supplement to the model of PURA that the government has launched. This model of PURA is more than a plan for "Providing Urban Amenities in Rural Areas"; it is a "Partnership of entrepreneurs, government administrators and the local populace for Urban Amenities within Rural Ambience". In contrast, in the present scheme of PURA, the government proceeds alone; it does not let others have co-ownership.

Only then will PURA grow rapidly, and not languish the way most satellite towns have. The driving force of connectivity is not enough; force multiplier of commercial investment too is limited in scope. Only when high-wage employees start residing inside PURA, and create a market for locally produced goods and services, will PURA grow rapidly, its development will be comprehensive, and investment in it profitable. With the induction of both organized businesses and their employees, PURA will see not marginal growth but total transformation, a transformation that will create educated employment with rural areas, curb rural-urban migration and prevent the satanic growth of slum-infested cities. Admittedly, this kind of PURA will succeed best when located not far from fast expanding cities. That is quite appropriate because, such villages need to grow as much as those in backward areas. Grant-in-aid schemes offer little scope for rapid growth particularly when the government is as cash strapped as it is. For profit-making schemes, the sky is the limit. That is why, the government should not fight shy of roping in private investors and try the profit-seeking model.

Spiritual Component

The President, Mr. Abdul Kalam, has been propagating the concept of PURA (Providing Urban amenities in Rural Areas), which he has made the core of his Vision 2020, with missionary zeal. During the 50th birthday celebrations of Mata Amritanandamayi (Amman), the President told the assembled CEOs: "I explained to her (Amma) the village development strategies of Providing Urban facilities in Rural Areas (PURA), consisting of four connectivites: Physical, electronic, knowledge and economic connectivity to enhance the prosperity of clusters of villages in the rural areas. Amman listened patiently and when I finished, turned to me with a smile and told me that something basic was missing. She went on to explain the rich culture and civilisational heritage of thousands of years that our country is proud of; the traditional bonds in a well-knit family system, where love, affection, mutual help and service are the prevailing emotions. Hence, the development effort in the rural area has to focus on the spiritual way of life."

Here is a new interpretation of Vision, a new meaning to the idea of vision 2020. As matter of interest, the young student volunteer who received me at the Kochi airport listened to my explanation of PURA and remarked that the scheme was essentially one that depends on partnership among business persons, social service agencies, the government and the public. For that reason, he suggested that the letter P in PURA should stand for Partnership. Evidently, the philosophy that Amma espouses has percolated down to the level of humble volunteers too. Taking up his suggestion, in my presentation to the CEOs, I described PURA as Partnership for Urban amenities with Rural Ambience. That kind of PURA appears to be an improvement on a top-down PURA that is visualised as one that merely Provides Urban amenities in Rural Areas.

Derivatives

PURA is an example of application of technology innovation for development. The tasks of technology are several: Reduce costs of production; offer higher levels of quality and utility; improve ecology; empower less skilled persons to produce more complex artefacts and services, and thereby raise their incomes. PURA satisfies all these conditions. PURA is also a complex operation; it requires the cooperation of a number of ministries both at the Centre and in the States. For all these reasons, before PURA can succeed, the government will have to reinvent itself. Getting the first one to take off in this manner is the toughest obstacle. Once one PURA takes off, the concept will roll on to fulfil the President's dream. Clearing the rural-urban divide is like jumping across a ditch: Jump fast enough, you are on a new path to unprecedented prosperity; jump short you fall into the ditch! More education and public pressure are required before PURA can take off. Let us hope that this alternative Vision will materialize, and make our villages look like those in Europe.

5

PURA—A Neo-Gandhian Approach to Development

RUDDAR DATT

Dr. A.P.J. Abdul Kalam, ever since he became the President of India has been advocating his Vision 2020, and, to eradicate poverty from India, he has been emphasizing the adoption of PURA (Providing Urban Amenities in Rural Areas). In his address to the Food Security Summit on 5th February 2004, he outlined the concept and strategy of PURA as the lever of economic upliftment of the villages. India currently has 260 million people living below the poverty line. The GDP growth has been on the average 6 per cent per annum during the last decade. It has to be gradually increased up to 10% and to be sustained for several years. Then it is possible for India get the status of a developed nation.

INTEGRATED ACTION

To achieve this, the roadmap involves integrated action

on the following five areas:

(i) Agriculture and food processing—The country should target for 360 million tonnes of food and agricultural production by 2020. Other areas of agriculture and agro-food processing would bring prosperity to rural people and speed up economic growth.

(ii) Reliable and quality electric power for all parts of the country.

(iii) Education and health care for all.

(iv) Expansion of information and communication technology to rural areas to promote education and create national wealth.

(v) Development of strategic sectors—growth in nuclear technology, space technology and defence technology.

All these areas have to be developed into mission such as: Networking of rivers, availability of high quality uninterrupted power, Providing Urban amenities in Rural Areas (PURA), Second Green Revolution, Information and Communication Technology (ICT) transforming into knowledge products and tourism.

PURA MODEL

PURA model involves four connectivities: Physical, electronic, knowledge and thereby leading to economic connectivity to enhance the prosperity of cluster of villages in the rural areas.

Under *physical connectivity*, a group of 15 to 25 villages will be linked to each other by road. These villages connected by roads will also have a ring road so that each one them can make use of it. Besides roads, provision of electricity and transport facilities have also been included.

Second is *digital connectivity* which aims to link villages with modern telecommunication and information technology services, e.g. Public call offices, cyber cafes, etc.

Thirdly, *knowledge connectivity* tries to establish on every 5 to 7 kms, of the circular ring road a school, a higher education centre, a hospital, etc.

Fourthly, *economic connectivity* aims to establish within this group of villages good marketing facilities so that all the commodities and services of daily use can be procured and the rural people can sell their produce in these markets.

THREE TYPES OF PURA

Depending upon the region and the state of present development, PURA can be classified into three different categories, namely, Type A, Type B and Type C—PURA clusters. The characteristics of these types are:

Type A cluster is situated close to urban area but has sparsely spread infrastructure and no connectivity.

Type B cluster is situated close to urban area but has sparsely spread infrastructure and no connectivity.

Type C cluster located far interior with no infrastructure, no connectivity and no basic amenities.

At the CEO Summit organised on the occasion of the Fifteeth birthday celebrations of Mata Amritanandamayi (Amma), President A.P.J. Abdul Kalam said: "PURA is one of the mechanisms which will be utilized for transforming our villages into productive economic zones." The Prime Minister in his Independence Day (2003) message announced the launching of 5,000 PURAs. Obviously, these are 5,000 Rural Development Blocks in the country. Each block has a population of 1,00,000. In the current Tenth Plan, the per capita investment is around Rs. 20,000 of which the Public sector accounts for nearly 50 per cent. This would imply that the public sector component of PURA for 5,000 Rural Development Block would of the order of Rs. 5,00,000 crores, i.e. at the rate Rs. 100 crore per PURA. The PURA is a Vision 2020 project and has to be spread over three five years plans to that an investment Rs. 100 crores is made in each development block or cluster.

GOVERNMENT ACTION ON THE PURA MODEL

The NDA Union Cabinet in its meeting on 20th January 2004 has accorded in principle approval for the execution of PURA within the existing gross budgetary support for bridging the rural-urban divide and achieving balanced socio-economic development. The Government envisages developments of over 4,000 rural clusters located in backward regions. A sum of Rs. 3 crores for each cluster has been provided and thus, Rs. 12,000 crores will be spent on the development of 4,000 PURAs.

ASSESSMENT OF PURA MODEL OF RURAL DEVELOPMENT

It was Mahatma Gandhi who underlined the exploitation of rural society by its urban counterpart. Gandhi wrote in Village Swaraj: "The British have exploited India through its cities. The latter have exploited the villages. The blood of the villages is the cement with which the edifice of the cities to run once again in the blood vessels of villages." (p. 25) As a policy statement, Gandhi stated: "The cities are capable of taking care of themselves. It is the villages we have to turn to." (p. 26) Gandhi to develop a harmonious relationship between the cities and villages categorically mentioned: "It is only when the cities realize the duty of making an adequate return to the villages for the strength and sustenance which they derive from them, instead of selfishly exploiting them, that a healthy and moral relationship between the two will spring up." (p. 29).

There is no doubt that the planning process did make an effort to develop the villages through community development projects. Irrigation facilities were enlarged and green revolution did provide an opportunity to the rural people to increase their share in national and per capita income, but still the rural-urban divide continues and there is a migration of population from rural to urban areas. Urban population which was 17.3 per cent of the total in 1951, has increased to 27.8 per cent in 2001. In absolute terms, as against 62 million persons living in urban areas in 1951, the numbers crowding in them have shot up to 285 million—an increase by 357 per cent. This has created problems of congestion and growth of slums

The objective of PURA is propel economic development without population transfers. To put in the words of late Prof. A.M. Khusro: Instead of moving human beings where infrastructure exists, it is better to take infrastructure to villages where human beings live. The PURA concept is the response to the need for creating social and economic infrastructure which can create a conducive climate for investment by the private sector to invest in rural areas.

But a mere provision of Rs. 3 crores per cluster against the need for Rs. 100 crores is too meagre. The best way to shelve a proposal is to accept it in principle and make a modicum of investment towards its implementation. Such a move is likely to kill the proposal. In fact, there was need for giving a more serious thought to the proposal and to support it to achieve success. Perhaps the democratic compulsions might have compelled the Government to announce bringing within its fold 4,000 Rural Development Blocks (or clusters) out of a total 7,000 and thus, extending its reach to nearly 57 per cent of the rural population in the backward areas. But such a thin layer of the investment as proposed by the Cabinet is not going to achieve the objectives of PURA.

A PRAGMATIC APPROACH

A more pragmatic approach would have been to select nearly 600 blocks in the backward areas and invest at least Rs. 25 crores per block to provide the needed infrastructure to Block Development Committee during the Tenth Plan, the remaining 35 per cent and 40 per cent should be provided in the Eleventh and the Twelfth Plan. Those states which promise to provide 20 per cent out of their revenues should receive 80 per cent grant from the Central Government. This would have necessitated to Centre to contribute Rs. 20 crores and with the present level of support of Rs. 12,000 crores, the PURA concept could have made a dent in developing the backward regions.

Secondly, the PURA proposal envisages three types—A, B and C. Type C being in the interior required much greater initial push, type B relatively less and type A can attract even private sector investment. Government should, therefore, develop a vision 2020 for the PURA development clusters and grade the degree of financial and other support consistent with the level of development achieved in a particular cluster. To overcome inertia, we need a big push and if the process begins to move, relatively lesser effort is needed to give it a momentum. Thus, a higher level of state support is need for Type C cluster.

Ongoing programmers of rural development can be re-oriented so that roads, electricity and water are made available. Once the social overheads are created, it will be possible to attract private sector investment. It is abundantly clear that private sector invests only in areas and projects which yield a high rate of return. It will, therefore, hesitate to move in the remote interior clusters unless the Government provides necessary infrastructural support and some incentives for the purpose.

For implementation of PURA, there is need for an Apex body under the chairmanship of the Deputy Chairman, Planning Commission. Each state should have a state level PURA Corporation which would be composed of representatives from small scale industry, financial institution, co-operatives, technical persons and representatives of panchayats, etc., roadmap for rural development of the state. The combined effort of the different participants in the PURA mission alone can assure its success. The Regional model as proposed in the PURA model may not be very helpful, since we do not have Regional Planning Boards but do have State Planning Boards.

DEMAND SIDE CONSTRAINTS

The major impediment to the PURA mission will be the on demand side. This can be achieved by undertaking such activities which create wage employment and thus, enlarge demand potential of the rural population. If PURA can become a catalyst for another green revolution in the backward rural areas in the less prosperous states, the Vision 2020 of the President to achieve a food production of 400 million tones can be achieved. For this purpose, it is necessary to develop synergy among the different constituents in the fulfilment of the PURA mission. Only then can we have the dream of development of rural India without population transfers realized.

Although PURA draws its inspiration from the Gandhian model of development which emphasis rural development as a fundamental postulate, yet in the prescription, it is neo-Gandhian in the sense, that it intends to bring rural regeneration with the avowed objective of taking modern technology and modern amenities to the rural areas. In this sense, it does not enter into the controversy of labour-intensive *versus* capital-intensive measures. However, it does emphasize the enlargement of employment as the sole objective to make use of rural manpower in various development activities. In this sense, it does not think of a second grade status for rural citizens and thus can become more acceptable to them. In other words, the PURA model attempts a reconciliation between employment and GDP growth objectives.

6

PURA : Towards a Sustainable Society

K. VENKATASUBRAMANIAN

INTRODUCTION

PURA is simply; Providing Urban amenities in Rural Areas; or, more aptly, Partnership for combining Urban amenities with Rural Ambience. Pura can be implemented by everyone. PURA can be implemented as a profit-making partnership too by industry interested in public welfare. Venture capitalists will underwrite the pre-operative costs of the project. Rurbanisers (a collection of town planners, service providers and social activists) will organize high quality urban amenities in rural areas. The Government has a major role also. Government administrators will initiate the process and regulate (not control) the same once it is implemented. In particular, PURA will be implemented not as the usual grant-in-aid rural development scheme but as a bankable, profit-making, commercial venture. PURA was conceptualized by observing that a city generates large number of high-paid jobs, all in the non-farm sector, whereas the same size population distributed over a number of villages has few jobs to offer, and wallows in poverty. That difference occurs because the city has a large market the like of which villages do not support. In turn, cities support a large market, and villages do not only because cities enjoy high connectivity, and villages do not offer that facility.

CONNECTIVITY CIRCLE

Our eminent Rashtrapathi Dr. A.P.J. Abdul Kalam has argued for the need for a variety of connectivities cogently.

(a) Physical connectivity of roads and transport;

(b) Economic connectivity of banking, commerce, insurance and warehousing;

(c) Knowledge connectivity of schools, colleges and vocational education;

(d) Societal connectivity of hospitals, recreation centres, places of worship; and

(e) Electronic connectivity that encompasses the entire space.

PURA aims to establish all these connectivities in as ample a measure as cities have. It is initiated through a two stage process:

(a) Ringing a loop of villages by a road, and linking that road to a nearby city.

(b) Running fast and frequent bus services on those roads.

The ring road is so devised that, on an average, all points are within 15 minutes of one another. Obviously, the faster the bus service, the larger the number of villages that will be served, and the larger the population that will be linked, and the larger the size of the market that will be supported. Hence, bus lanes should be designed for fast and smooth flow with no encroachments to impede vehicles. The link road that connects the ring road to the city will further enhance the connectivity of the rural space, and make it even more valuable commercially. Once the bus service comes into operation, any facility that is established at any point on the ring road will acquire a large customer base from all connected villages. Many services that currently flourish only in large towns and cities can now operate profitably on the ring road. In consequence, many new jobs will be created, and they will be in the non-farm sector too.

The ring-road configuration has been chosen because, compared to all other geometries, it needs minimum length of infrastructure. It can be shown that compared to the conventional rectangular grid or radial town plans, there will be a saving of at least fifty per cent. Both for this reason, and because rural space costs little, moving urban expansion to the space alongside the ring road becomes more economical than locating the same expansion on the outskirts of a congested city. In the bargain, rural-urban migration becomes unnecessary, and cities too benefit with less congestion, and less price-inflation.

EMPLOYMENT MULTIPLIER

The essence of employment creation is multiplication, not mere addition; that is, every job created in the secondary sector should be multiplied several-fold in the service sector. Unfortunately, employees tend to reside in the city and commute to the new jobs created in the satellite town. Then, job creation occurs in the satellite town but job multiplication remains with the city with the result most of the economic gains of investment in the satellite town flow back to the city and do not remain in the satellite town. As a remedy, PURA will have a rule that all employers house their employees inside PURA itself. Employees do not have to commute at all because they can now reside within walking distance from place of work. Such co–location of business space and residential space is a particular facility that the ring road offers, and other designs do not.

ECONOMIC COMPONENTS

In economic terms, PURA has three distinct components:

(a) The ring and link roads: These roads will have to be constructed up front, but the investment is safe because these roads will ever remain a permanent asset in whatever way PURA may shape up.

(b) Fast and frequent bus services plus acquiring land for development: These expenses too will have to be incurred up front, but large returns can be expected as bus services will increase land prices enormously.

(c) Establishing a full range of urban amenities like schools, hospitals, shopping malls, recreation centres and the like. These facilities can start small, and expand gradually as demand increases.

IMPLEMENTATION STRATEGIES

PURA may then be implemented as follows:

(a) Rurbanisers—a partnership of town planners, farmers, venture capitalists, social activists and bankers—choose a few ring road alignments, close to an expanding city.

(b) Venture capitalists select the alignment that is most profitable after taking into account the price the farmers demand.

(c) The state constructs the ring and link roads.

(d) Venture capitalists organise a Road Show inviting a comprehensive mix of service providers and businessmen—on one condition, that they lease enough land to house both their business and residences for employees.

(e) Banks offer low–cost credit to employers to start their business, and to employees to build their own houses.

Assuming that the ring and link roads will each be about 30 kms in length, the first step of constructing the ring and link roads will cost the government about Rs. 40-50 crores. That one-time cost can be met from the Prime Minister's Gram Sadak Yojana. Better still, the cost may be met from bank loans with the Rural Development Ministry guaranteeing interest repayment of Rs. 3-4 crores annually. The Ministry may recover that cost by levying a betterment fee on the land that will now develop on either side of the ring road. Alternately, a toll may be collected from vehicles.

The speculative risk of acquiring land for development can be reduced drastically if the space is not purchased outright but taken on long lease, say, for 99 years as was the case in Hong Kong. Farmers, from states as wide apart as Tamil Nadu, Maharashtra, Punjab and Karnataka, have expressed strong interest in a scheme that will guarantee them twice the income they now get by sharecropping (with a residential plot and a built-up shop thrown in as a bonus). In addition, they may also be given vouchers for concessional education and hospital services. In that case, farmers benefit not only from enhanced inflation – protected income but will also get facilities that they can only dream of at present.

Venture Capitalists too benefit because they now have to risk not the full cost of purchasing land but only the cost of servicing these commitments to the farmers, and that too only till PURA takes off. Then, as little as Rs. 8-10 crores of venture capital could suffice to launch a PURA. Charging a modest rent of Rs. 30-50 per square metre per year could yield attractive returns to venture capitalists. Ultimately, only commercial service providers can make PURA succeed. In their case, risks are nominal : they need invest no more than what is needed to meet current demand. They can increase their investment gradually keeping in pace with the growth in demand.

CONDUCIVE FACTORS

For PURA to succeed, the following precautions should be taken:

(a) Enough provision should be made right at the start to allow for the future expansion of the ring and link roads.

(b) As a corollary, the expansion space should at all times be kept free of all encroachments.

(c) All employees should be induced to stay in PURA. For that purpose, it should be a precondition that all employers rent enough space to house their employees.

(d) Investments should be made according to normal urban standards, and not according to the prevailing sub-standard rural practice.

Apart from the reason of its rural location, PURA is economical because the ring design cuts all infrastructure lengths by fifty per cent or more. However, that advantage will be lost if PURA is over expanded, and space farther than a few hundred metres from the ring road is developed. Even with that limitation, a typical PURA can grow to accommodate several hundred thousand people without losing its rural ambience, namely, freedom from commuting to work, large residences, ample recreation space, social cohesion, and quality ecology with local water harvesting and waste recycling.

UNIQUENESS OF THE MODEL

This model of PURA can be launched with an (ultimately recoverable) annual contribution of Rs. 3–5 crores for meeting the interest cost of constructing ring/link roads, plus a venture capital of Rs. 6–10 crores for meeting the expenses of leasing land and running buses till both become profitable. PURA differs in five ways the scheme sanctioned by the Central Government in which over 4000 PURAs are being funded at a cost of Rs. 3 crores each. One, government's contribution is not a grant but a recoverable investment. Two, this scheme is a partnership: the state initiates but ultimately, private enterprise takes over. Three, the government scheme confines PURA to the most backward rural areas; the model described here will operate in the proximity of growing cities. Four, the number of PURAs will increase gradually, based on economic profitability, and not start with a bang. Five, this is a business enterprise dependent on marketing the space alongside the ring road as a more desirable alternative to the expansion of a city in the vicinity. Hence, it is best left to an autonomous corporation, and not treated as a scheme of social welfare to be handled departmentally by Block Development Officers.

Currently, urban population in India is expanding by about 10-12 million a year. Vision 2020 should be for PURA to capture at least ten per cent of that expansion at the start, and the whole of it in course of time. Let us stop RURAL exodus by PURA so that all urban amenities go to the villages and people also will go back. Did not our great father of the Nation, the Mahatma request us to go back to the villages. Let us do it now at least.

7

PURA: An Academic Angle

P. JEGADISH GANDHI

The strength and stability of Indian economy inevitably depend upon the development of rural sector, since nearly 70 percent of the people in India are dependent for their living on agriculture and allied sectors. The pace and poise of economic development in India naturally hinge on the 'total' development of rural society. In post-Independence era both Governmental projects and voluntary agencies have failed in its bid to shake-up the shackles of the old agrarian set-up partly due to its piecemeal character and partly due to the lack of active involvement of rural people. A change in agrarian relations, rural production lines, consumption patterns and social dialectics affect the village system. Even today "India lives in its villages". Rural development can be defined many ways. "What is crucial is that it is defined by rural people themselves or by their organization. To define 'rural development' we need to invert the process by first defining problems and issues of the rural areas with the rural people; secondly, there is a need to define the goals of the future state and this will have to take into account the problems and issues that have been raised; and third, we come to a generalized understanding of 'rural development'." (*Report of the Asian Rural Economy Consultation*, 1993.)

RURAL COMMUNITARIANISM

In *Indian Economic Thought* (1977), Professor B.N. Ganguli has presented a critique of the historical rural and urban economic philosophy. Rural communitarianism, "as a species of economic philosophy, had, at any rate in India, a wide sweep and included many strands and levels of social thought. The starting-points were, in fact, those elements of western economic philosophy, which deployed against *laissez-faire* and capitalistic industrialism and were specifically oriented towards ruralism, as contrasted with urban industrialism. Rural communitarianism was not necessarily an anti-modernist throw-back. Indeed, while modern economic progress was admired, it was recognized that it was of the essence of economic progress to eliminate the excesses of wealth and poverty, the "alienation" between man and man and between town and country, which urban industrialism generates, so that the countryside becomes a peripheral "hinterland", an appendage struggling to adjust to the values created by an urban civilization, itself a product of urban industrialism."

"Towards the end of the nineteenth century, an important section of the Indian intelligentsia began to think of rural communitarianism as an alternative path of development. What Rammohun Roy had in mind was a process of modernization that involved the vast masses of the population, through whom the growth impulse could travel outward and forward on a massive scale.... Gandhiji's attempt to build a rural communitarian society adapted to modern ideas of cooperation and community service, but resting on an old traditional structure purged of its existing evils, was criticized on the ground that the "ancient plan" was individualistic to the core and not adapted to corporate effort of any kind.... On one level of thought, rural communitarianism was a protest against certain values associated with western industrialism: materialism, hedonism, acquisitiveness and class conflict threatening social stability."

RURAL-URBAN DIVIDE

The most important class conflict in the poor countries of the world today is not between labour and capital. Nor is it between foreign and national interest. It is between the rural classes and the urban classes. The rural sector contains most of the poverty, and most of the low-cost sources of potential advance; but the urban sector contains most of the articulateness, organization and power. So the urban classes have been able to "win" most of rounds of the struggle with the countryside; but in so doing they have made the development process needlessly slow and unfair.... This huge welfare gap is demonstrably inefficient, as well as inequitable (Michael Lipton, 1977). Rural and urban development complement each other: Cities choke when rural development fails, and villages stagnate when urban development is distorted. We are witnessing both problems in India (P.V. Indiresan). The World Bank Report on India *(Sustaining Reform, Reducing Poverty,* 2003) as also the UNDP's Human Development Report, 2003 have expressed grave concern over the widening inter-state disparities and the growing urban-rural divide in India. If the widening regional disparities and the growing rural-urban divide are not arrested and reversed soon, they will not only continue to pull down the overall economic growth rate, but also lead to serious social strife in the country. It is time policy-makers view the situation with a new sense of urgency and initiated measures to contain the damage (S.D. Naik).

KALAM'S RURAL ECONOMICS

Dr. A.P.J. Abdul Kalam was neither a student of economics nor trained in applied economic apparatus. But he had a first-hand understanding of the global and national economic trends based on his jobs, observations and experiences. As a practical economic thinker, Dr. Kalam has a grand vision of a "developed India" by 2020 using economic principles and practices. He belonged to a new brand called, *Visionary economists.* His holistic economic vision of India and for India has to endure as a possibility in future when our feet become stronger and we are able to see a resurgent nation far ahead. Dr. Kalam would qualify to be an economist in the eyes of the great neo-classical English economist and the propounder of the popular Welfare definition of Economics, Alfred Marshall has stated in his masterpiece, *Principles of Economics* (1890): "The fact is that nearly all founders of modern economics, were men of gentle and sympathetic tempos touched with the enthusiasm of humanity. They cared little for wealth for themselves, they cared much for its wide diffusion among the masses of the people."

Dr. Kalam had the benefit of discussions with a wide range of people in society: well-educated housewives, professionals, social scientists, historians, psychologists, economists, administrators, politicians, youngsters and ordinary people. This cross-sectional interaction enabled Dr. Kalam to find out that "Everywhere there was a genuine interest to act, to break the vicious circle of pessimism and inaction." Against this backdrop, he pinpointed that "While aggregated economic indicators are important, it does not make sense to achieve a 'developed' status without a major and continuing upliftment of all Indians who exist today and of the many millions who would be added in the years to come. They should all have a secure and enjoyable 'present' and also be in a position to look forward to a better 'future'. Such a developed India is what we are looking for Gandhiji emphasized that only when we have wiped the tears from the faces of all Indians, have we truly arrived as a Nation. It is that kind of deep and unshakable commitment to the well-being of India." This is what we may call Kalam's message of genuine-native and real-development.

HOME-GROW MODEL OF DEVELOPMENT

Dr. Kalam is categorical about development modelling

for our country. He asserted that: "We must regain our broad outlook and draw upon our heritage and wisdom to enrich our lives. The fact that we advance technologically does not preclude spiritual development. We need to home-grow our own model of development based on our inherent strengths. Progress is rapid wherever there is an efficient administrative set-up, a high level of education and minimum political interference in development activity. Development is a security—centric phenomenon from poverty to food security, social security and thereafter national security. Action in five core areas—agriculture and food processing, supply of electricity, education and healthcare, information technology and strategic sector—properly *integrated,* would lead to food, economic, social and national security. A strong *partnership* between the research and development institutions, universities, industry and the community as a whole with the government departments and agencies will be essential to accomplish the vision. The key to success lies in *connectivity.* The development of education and healthcare will yield the benefits of smaller families and a more efficient workforce. It is the key to employability and social development. Improvements in the agricultural sector, including that of food processing, would lead to food security, employment opportunities and rapid economic growth. Growth in the information technology sector would assist rapid economic growth as well as play 'an important part in speeding up development. Electric power provides energy security so crucial for all sectors. The strategic sector has a direct impact on industry, sustaining growth and technological strength For balanced development, all the five areas are of importance."

The vision of a developed India can be realized only if we recognize that wealth generation and wealth protection are two sides of the same coin. A nation's wealth represents the sweat and hard work of its people. This is possible only with an *integrated approach* towards development. An integrated mission approach would permit interweaving of measures to generate wealth with similar steps for wealth protection. This is the hallmark of a developed country and hence the key to a developed India *(Ignited minds).* Overall, people, economy, strategic strengths and ability to sustain and improve on these over very long periods of time in the future —it would appear that mastering of technologies is the key task to which the country and its people have to give importance. This can be considered to be the very essence of development *(India 2020)*.

A serious study of Dr. Kalam's "stand-up" society points to what we may call neo-Swadeshi revolution in social dynamics of India. It is based on inherent indigenous, culture and contemporary impactional societal influences, i.e., maximising the Indianness in development programmes to reduce the foreign dependency syndrome. It is a critical turning point from the 'catch up', strategy that is adopted in the development of developing countries even since the end of the Second World War. His vision of a "resurgent " Nation is a new development paradigm visualizing a different India by the turn of the first quarter of the 21st century.

RURAL CONNECTIVITY

In Dr. Kalam's development paradigm, the cord of 'Connectivity' is a strategic component in rural transformational mission mode. "Connectivity has two parts: "getting around" and "getting away". Till the end of the 19th century, getting around involved walking. People walked to work, to the market, to school, to everywhere else in the town. In the initial years of the 20th century, mass transportation, often in the form of underground metros, let cities grow in size and accommodate millions of people. Now, the car has taken over development implies that people will drive to work, to the market, to the school or to work, to the market, to school or for anything else (P.V. Indiresan).

Dr. Kalam in *India 2020* has explained the complementarity and supplementarity of rural and urban areas in a sequential picturesque way. "Over a period, a number of modern scientific and technological achievements have helped the rural areas well. They have also affected rural life-style, sometimes irreversibly. Modern fertilizer and agro-chemicals based high yield agriculture, health services, electricity, radio, television, bus services, agro-machinery and plastic footwear are a few examples. However, there has been a symmetry between the rural and urban areas. Since urban areas are centres of industrial and business activities and also seats of political power, many facilities for better life are first established there. The economies of scale would also be cited as being influential in people taking such decisions. Wealth begets wealth. Higher economic activity begets more economic activities and therefore more employment. Therefore, migration from rural areas begins. Many underemployed persons move to the other cities in search of a better life. Most cities are becoming unlivable as about 50 percent of their inhabitants live in slums or near-slum conditions, or live so far away that they tire themselves in commuting. Therefore, it is possible to connect clusters of villages through a nearly annular ring of roads, with traffic designed in such a way that movement from one village to another can be quick and convenient. This helps in many ways. Many agro-industries, services industries and even high tech concerns, can be relocated in such villages by moving a few government offices and providing special concessions for industries. Once the process starts, economic activities will take care of the rest. These clusters have to be managed in an imaginative fashion, involving local people, panchayats, business persons and the intelligentsia which will move in. The vision includes the building of many such clusters all over India."

INTER-REGIONAL INTEGRATION

The concept of 'growth people' first introduced by Perroux in 1955 is based on one simple truth: human activities must cluster together to generate internal and external economies. This may, however involve some social costs which can be minimized in due course through proper policy interventions. "A serviceable rural development programme in India must deal with the several aspects of the rural economy in an integrated fashion. An isolated agricultural development effort unrelated to, and unsupported by other kinds of rural policies would be doomed to failure almost surely (John P. Lewis, 1970). In the Indian context, two approaches have emerged towards integration of spatial units, namely villages. These are: the Growth Centre Approach as developed by Gadgil and Sen, and the Village Cluster Approach as developed by V.K.R.V. Rao and V.M. Rao. The former suggests a vertical integration between the hierarchy of human settlements i.e., villages and towns. It is assumed that such a link up will transmit to the lower point in the hierarchy growth impulses from the top growth centres. The latter, on the other hand, advocates a horizontal link-up among the villages themselves so that they support each other functionally as to make the cluster of village an economically viable unit. Of course, both approaches stress on linkages, backward and forward (Abdul Aziz, 1989). The concept of integration is also viewed as integration of low income segments with the rest of the rural community by ensuring them a better participation in the production process and a more equitable share in the benefits of development (FAO, Report, 1977).

PURA MODEL

Contextually, to bridge the rural-urban divide and achieve balanced socio-economic development, Dr. Kalam has formulated an alternative rural development programme called PURA, i.e. Providing Urban amenities in Rural Areas. In most of his writings and Presidential speeches, Dr. Kalam has invariably focused on this new rural development path and urged the policy-makers, industrialists, philanthropists and religious leaders to partake in the neo-rural reconstruction challenges. PURA is a strip of habitation about 500 metres wide on either side of ring road linking a loop of villages. Hence, every point in PURA will be within walking distance from open farms on one side and a modern road transport system on the other. Places of work will normally be within transports system on the other. Places of work will normally be within walking distance. It will have broad uncrowded

KALAM'S PURA MODEL

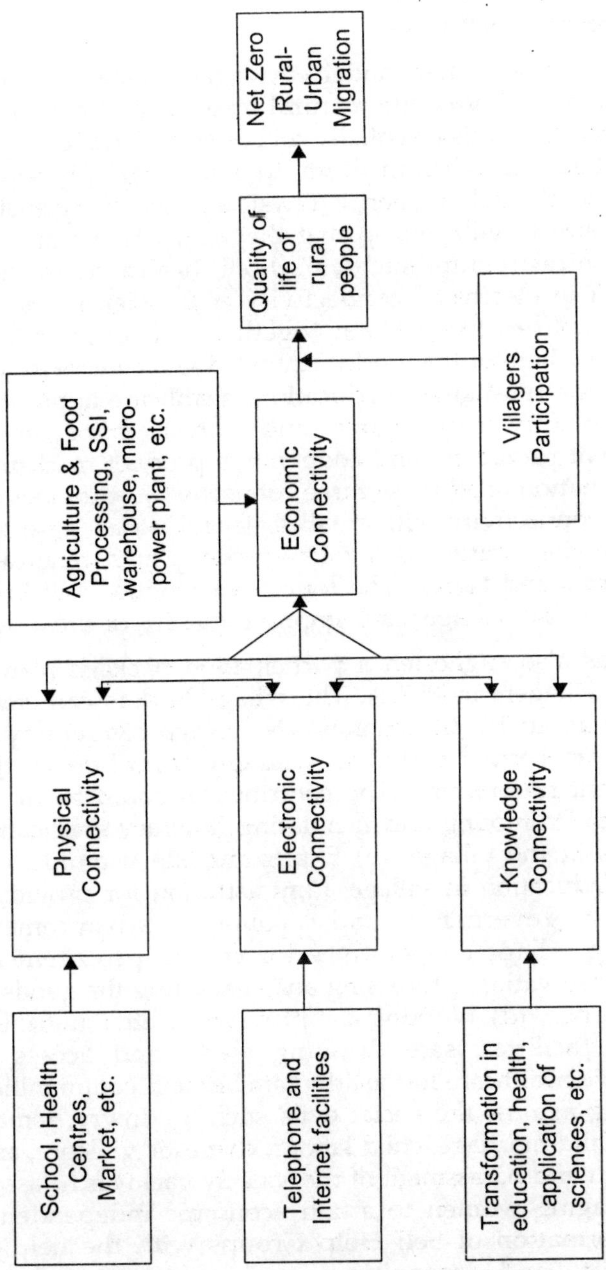

streets; gracious pathways.

Dr. Kalam's PURA model envisages habitat design to improve the quality of life in rural areas and also removes urban congestion. It is essentially conceived around four types of connectivities with the aim to speed up process of achieving total rural prosperity. Physical connectivity enables high mobility to villagers so that they can interact and use common infrastructure such as school, health centres and markets. The electronic connectivity with telephones and Internet facilities bring them together and interact with anyone anywhere in the world. Knowledge connectivity will transform the rural area in education, healthcare application of science for crop, water and forest management, environment protection and cooperative product marketing. The combination of all these three connectivities provides the economic connectivity with small-scale industries, agro and food processing, warehouses, micro-power plants, renewable energy farms and banks. The four connectivities will bring prosperity to the villages and improve quality of life.

He has also suggested a participation package plan of action for villagers in PURA. The village leaders can create awareness about PURA amongst the village community so that they can come forward to willingly contribute in this development programme. The contribution could be in the form of: (a) Promoting and facilitating illiteracy eradication campaigns in the village, (b) Explaining the usefulness of computer education in village administration for providing transparent governance and economic advancement, (c) Forming village cooperatives for central procurement, storage, preservation, processing and marketing the goods at attractive price, (d) Working for providing better nutrition, sanitation facilities, safe drinking water and access to reproductive healthcare for healthy families and communities, (e) Fighting against the social evils such as dowry, female foeticide, child marriage, child labour, domestic violence, and ill-treatment and harassment of the socially backward classes, (f) Encouraging women to attain economic independence through formation of Self Help Groups with the help of micro-credit and organising various skill training programmes, and (g) Facilitating the conservation of energy through effective utilization of solar power, recycling the waste for energy generation and management of water through rainwater harvesting, etc.

Statistically, Kalam's PURA model explains the rural people quality of life is supposed to be the function of four connectivities:

$$Qr = C\ (p, e, k, ec) \qquad \dots (1)$$

where Qr is the quality of life of rural people, p is the physical connectivity, e is the electronic connectivity, k is the knowledge connectivity and ec is the economic connectivity.

The low level of four connectivities in the rural economy results in more rural-urban migration. In order to improve quality of rural life assuming that the established connectivities in urban centres brings higher wage rate than the rural where low connectivities are witnesses:

$$Wu > Wr \qquad \dots (2)$$

In terms of the Harris-Todaro Model (1970)

$$W_u^e = \bar{w}m\ .\ Nm/Nu,\ (Nm/Nu) \leq 1 \qquad \dots (3)$$

Dr. Kalam's model (Eq. 1) suggests that the dynamics of 'four connectivity' does ensure the 'near zero net rural-urban migration', when the quality of life of rural people improves,

$$\Delta Qr = \Delta C\ (p, e, k, ec) \qquad \dots (4)$$

Again, where there is a participation of village community (v), the equation 4 will be,

$$\Delta Qr = \Delta C\ (p, e, k, ec) + v \qquad \dots (5)$$

ZERO NET RURAL-URBAN MIGRATION

The most of many rural-urban interactions is the synergistic role that agriculture plays in the development of the non-agricultural sector. From agriculture comes the supply of labour to industry and the surplus of food that allows a non-agricultural labour force to survive. These are the two fundamental resource flows from agriculture, and they lie at the heart of the structural transformation that occurs in most developing countries (Debraj Ray). The classic model of rural-urban migration is based on Harris and Todaro. The basic concept behind the model is that rural-urban migration will continue so long as the expected urban real income is more than real wage rate in the agricultural sector. "Migration today must be seen as major contributing factor to the ubiquitous phenomenon of urban surplus labour and a force which continues to exacerbate already serious urban unemployment problems caused by a growing economic and structural imbalance between urban and rural area" (Todaro). More literate and higher educated are migrating to the metropolitan cities than the illiterates. The push factors may be important in the case of illiterates, but the positive push factors may be important in the case of illiterates, but the positive push and pull factors are important in the case of the educated (D.L. Narayana). In fact, the net rural-urban migration (decadal), in India registered a considerable decline even in absolute terms. Around 19.73 million people were estimated as net migrants over the decade 1971-81. This figure decelerated to 12.73 million during 1981-91, reducing its relative share in total increase in the urban population, from 39.40 percent to 22.62 percent. The decline in the growth rate of urban population during the last decade can, therefore, be attributed mainly to the decline in the net rural-urban migration (Arup Mitra) .

Dr. Kalam's PURA model is based on an unique equilibrium conditionality, i.e. achieving "near Zero net rural-urban migration" through the dynamics of "connectivity". "The fact that there is net migration from villages to cities indicates that they offer more opportunities, and the only way to equalize the flow is to develop the rural areas and bring life there on par with that in the cities. This means providing rural areas with the amenities that are currently available only in cities. This would generate employment on the same scale, and at the same level, as in the cities in the rural areas too. The other challenge would be to provide these benefits at a small fraction of the financial social, cultural and ecological costs the cities have to bear. It is the expectation that this combination of generating employment bearing in mind environmental factors will make rural areas as attractive as cities are, if not even more attractive. Then, rural development may be expected to prevent, if not actually reverse, rural-urban migration."

PURA Model may be illustrated as follows:

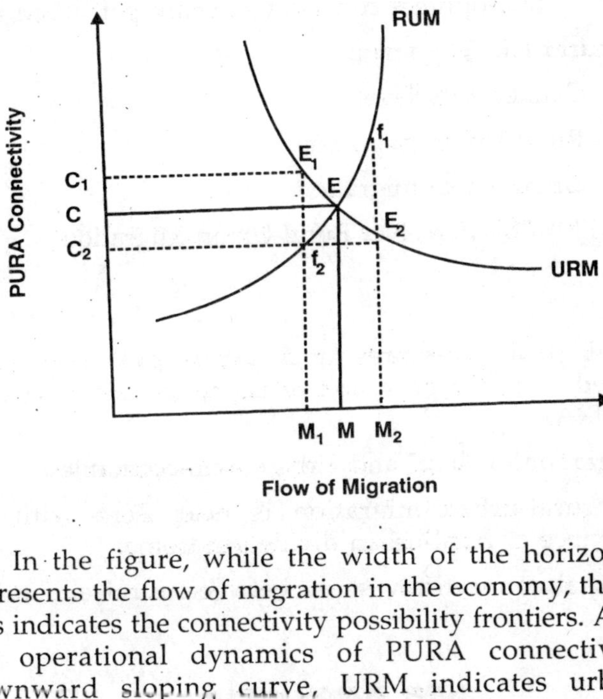

In the figure, while the width of the horizontal axis represents the flow of migration in the economy, the vertical axis indicates the connectivity possibility frontiers. Assuming the operational dynamics of PURA connectivity, the downward sloping curve, URM indicates urban-rural migration trends and the upward sloping curve RUM describes rural-urban migration trends. We can visualize 3 scenarios out of the given variables.

Scenario I: At point E_1

OC_1—High connectivity level

M_1E_1—High Urban-Rural migration

M_1f_1—Low Rural-Urban migration

Result: Greater Urban-Rural divide
Over-optimal connectivity share per urban unit.

Scenario II: At point E_2

OC_2—Low connectivity level

M_2E_2—Low Urban-Rural migration

M_2f_2—High Rural-Urban migration

Result: Greater Rural-Urban divide
Sub-optimal connectivity share per urban unit.

Scenario III: At point E

OC—Connectivity level

EM—Rural-Urban migration

EM—Urban-Rural migration

OC=EM=EM=Zero Net Rural-Urban Migration.

Result

Rural push pressures and urban pull forces are neutralized with the provision of urban amenities in rural areas (PURA).

Integration of Rural and Urban socio-economies.

Net rural-urban migration is near Zero with the disappearance of rural urban divide syndrome.

Optimal connectivity share between rural and urban units.

NEW RURAL INDIA

Dr. Kalam visualized that "The development of the nation requires enhancement of economic connectivity of the villages. Out of the 6 lakh villages in the country about 50,000 PURA complexes would emerge. The basic strategy for societal and economic transformation of India towards its vision as a developed society by 2020 would be a strong focus on providing urban amenities in rural areas in most effective and creative manner. The PURA has to be a business proposition economically viable and managed by entrepreneurs and small scale industrialists, as it involves education, health, power generation, transport and management. Government's support should be available in empowering such management agencies in providing initially economic support and finding the right type of management structure and the leaders to manage. What is the type of farming to be chosen, area under cultivation, water management, production, food processing and marketing is a task of paramount effort. Technological institutions could make a simulation model of PURA with various connectivities and conduct sensitivity analysis of various inputs on collaboration with the Ministry of Rural Development. Marking the 57th Independence Day (15th August 2003), the Prime Minister A.B. Vajpayee has announced a bold policy decision that the PURA scheme is to be implemented in 5000 rural clusters across the country in the next five years. Orissa will have the unique honour of having the first fully Government initiated PURA. This has kindled many private agencies and NGOs to direct their efforts towards creating more PURAs which are economically viable and technologically sustainable. "It is in this respect that Dr. Kalam scores over professional planners whether they are in the bureaucracy or in politics. He is the first important person to emphasise the importance of connectivity. That mantra will integrate the Planning Commission's measures of development with the Prime Minister's desire for rapid growth and Dr. Kalam's dream for truly developed India" (P.V. Indiresan). This is a major singular success for Dr. Kalam in pathwaying for new rural India. PURA provides a seamless connection and movement of molecules (people), atoms (material) and electron (knowledge). Overall, rural development is not only a process, a method, a programmer, but also a movement in our country.

entrepreneurs, individual, cottage industries and livelihood [illegible] education, health, [illegible] generation, transport, and the relevant Government support [illegible] connectivity, such as research agencies [illegible] [illegible] sugar and [illegible] [illegible] and [illegible] the type of [illegible] chosen [illegible] micro irrigation, water management, production, storage and marketing [illegible] [illegible] technological interventions could make [illegible] model of PURA with physical connectivity, and [illegible] sensitivity analysis of various inputs in collaboration with the Ministry of Rural Development. [illegible] (15th August 2003), the Prime Minister [illegible] announced [illegible] that the PURA scheme to be implemented in 5000 rural clusters [illegible] country in the next five years. [illegible] [illegible] Government and PURA. This has kindled many private agencies and NGOs to direct their efforts towards creating [illegible] PURAs which are economically viable and technologically sustainable. It is in this respect that [illegible] [illegible] [illegible] [illegible] integrated [illegible] Planning [illegible] development with the Prime Minister's [illegible] and [illegible] [illegible] major [illegible] [illegible] rural [illegible] connection and [illegible] and electronic (knowledge). [illegible] development [illegible] [illegible]

PART III

POST-PURA SCENARIO: TRANSFORMING RURAL "REALITIES"

8

Connecting Rural India: Village Resource Centres

M.S. SWAMINATHAN

RURAL KNOWLEDGE REVOLUTION

Three significant developments in recent months provide hope for taking the power of the Internet and the space age to the country's 600,000 villages by August 15, 2007, which marks the 60th Anniversary of India's "tryst with destiny". First, a National Alliance has been formed by a wide range of civil society, industrial, and academic organisations to harness the power of partnership in achieving the goals of Mission 2007: every village a knowledge centre. Second, with support from Tata Trusts a Jamsetji Tata National Virtual Academy for Rural Prosperity has been established at the M.S. Swaminathan Research Foundation for training and electing one million rural women and men as Fellows of the Academy. They will be the torch-bearers of the rural knowledge revolution. Third, the Prime Minister launched the Indian Space Research Organisation—MSSRF Village Resource Centre programme on October 18, 2004. This programme will concentrate on helping rural women, men and children meet their basic needs in education, nutrition, health, drinking and irrigation water, agriculture and markets.

Mission 2007 needs for its success appropriate public policy support. The policy support needed for sustaining this movement has been discussed among partners of the National Alliance Partners for achieving synergy between technology and public policy. At present villages in India are hardly connected. Almost all the telecom operators see rural connectivity as a loss-making proposition. They want heavy subsidies to provide minimum connectivity in the villages. At the same time, immense infrastructure, in the form of optical fibre and towers, has been built up in India over the last 20 years. Thanks to the efforts of the Department of Telecommunications and Bharat Sanchar Nigam Limited and to some extent the private operators, this infrastructure is not limited to cities and big towns, but has gone deep into the smallest towns, including almost all talk headquarter towns. Also inexpensive wireless technologies exist to extend connectivity from these fiber optic cable linked towns to most of the villages.

CAPACITY BUILDING

However, if left to the telecom operators focussed on the urban areas, this connectivity will take years. The rural areas cannot wait. There are smaller companies, NGOs and other outfits focussed on providing services in rural areas. These organisations should be enabled to use the existing infrastructure (fibre backbones and towers) to provide telecom and Internet connectivity in the villages. The owners of the infrastructure should get a share of the call charges. Over 30,000 exchanges have been connected by fibre. The STD-PCO model, redesigned to include an integrated ICT package including the Internet, will be economically sustainable. Both last mile technology and first mile delivery need concurrent attention. Priority should go to effective use of the already available infrastructure, particularly with BSNL. This will call for some additional investment. Maximising the benefits of the fibre infrastructure available today with the active participation of BSNL should be a major aim of public policy and investments. Capacity building of ICT-SHGs (Self-help Group) and human resource development are essential for success.

ALLIANCE PARTNERS

The Jamsetji Tata National Virtual Academy for Rural Prosperity established at MSSRF can play a vital role in this area. It can organise training programmes in the area of distance education and help enroll at least one woman and man as Fellows of the Academy from each village, with the help of alliance partners. There is need for investment in creating databases relevant to rural needs. The viability, sustainability and scalability of the rural families. Panchayati raj institutions should be mobilised. The ICT Knowledge Centre could be located either in a village school or Panchayat building (i.e., public spaces), so that there is social inclusion in access. Private sector industry can play a major role in linking rural products with markets. This will help to mitigate farmers' distress.

BUSINESS MODEL

Neither subsidy nor regulation has been able to get appropriate connectivity into the rural areas. Only a business model like that of STD-PCOs would make the telecom and Internet connectivity economically viable in rural areas. The smaller companies interested in providing services in rural India should be encouraged to use, for profit, business models and whatever last-mile technologies they chose to extend the connectivity to the villages. To help create viable business models, both cheap connectivity and cheap spectrum are essential.

TRAI recently brought out draft recommendations for unified license in which the concept of niche operators has been introduced for rural areas in particular. To ensure the efficacy of such effort even in the most backward areas, Government must mandate their use of the existing infrastructure at terms fixed by the regulator.

To make the model attractive initially, the charges for data transmission may be lower than voice, for a specific time-frame. Similarly, lower spectrum charges for a finite period of time may also be considered for the niche operators. They could also be wooed by avoiding large upfront payments and providing tax holiday for a limited period.

SOCIAL INFRASTRUCTURE CONNECTIVITY

Connectivity is, however, only the first step. What can the rural people do with computers and connectivity? The need is to strengthen education and extend health services in rural India. But going beyond that the key should be to revitalise the rural economy by creating sustainable rural micro-enterprises supported by micro-credit. "Education, health, nutrition and livelihoods for all" should be the ultimate goal of Mission 2007.

The rural economy can flourish if ICT are leveraged to create new livelihood opportunities. These could be in the area of agriculture, food processing, animal husbandry, fisheries, sericulture, handicrafts, and even in IT-based services (which rural India could provide to urban areas). Private sector and civil society organizations should be encouraged to develop ICT-based supply chain management systems to sell rural products.

Complex technology management must be relegated to the backend, handled by town and city-based organisations. The front-end in the villages must be easily manageable. There is need to invest in creating knowledge database relevant to rural needs. The content must be local and must use local languages. There should be provision for making available dynamic information for example about the weather and markets, as well as generic information about entitlements to government programmes, disaggregated by gender, age, class, and caste.

Essential services such as educational and healthcare can be delivered through ICT penetration in the rural areas. Government could install a few computers in the rural schools. Doctors from Government hospitals could offer on-line consultation particularly for women.

Need for Outsourcing

Rural people, especially the unemployed youth and women, should be considered assets in national development. The Government could decide as a policy priority to out-source functions such as digitization of land records, data entry operations, collation of local data and local resource mapping to the information kiosks run by self-help and community interest groups with the support of civil society organisation. Panchayati raj institutions could use connectivity to provide accountable and transparent local governance. Various government data of relevance to the public, including birth and death certificates, other registrations, and pension documentation could also be made on-line to facilitate usage. Outsourcing from urban to rural India would be a powerful method of bridging the rural-urban digital divide. This would also help to bridge the gender divide if women are enable to manage the rural knowledge centres.

SOCIAL MESSAGES

Relevant social messages in health education and governance related issues can be effectively disseminated through knowledge centres and information kiosks in rural areas. The Government should outsource designing and developing e-governance content and service to civil society and professional organizations that can benefit wider communities. A number of expert organizations in agriculture, nutrition, livelihoods, animal husbandry, post-harvest technology, health environmental issues, should be identified to support e-governance programmes. A civil society group should be constituted to monitor the e-governance policies. Such a group can advise the Government on appropriate methods of automating government processes and offering ICT enabled services and applications for rural communities. A low interest rate lending to rural entrepreneurs, self-help groups, common interest groups and nominees if panchayati raj institution to establish knowledge centres and information kiosks should be considered such loans can be issued via banking institution such as NABARD, SBI, etc. to encourage rural entrepreneurship. A venture capital fund may also be established.

The task of taking the benefits of the Internet and space age to 600,000 villages by August 15, 2007, may appear to be formidable one. However, seemingly impossible tasks can be achieved by harnessing the power of partnership and by bringing about synergy between demonstrated by the Green Revolution of the 1960. The initiative launched by our Prime Minister marks the beginning of a bright chapter in India's tryst with destiny.

NETWORKED VILLAGE RESOURCE CENTRE

Inaugurating the VRC project via INSAT link from New Delhi, the Prime Minister Dr. Manmohan Singh said the Department of Space had become a role model for other institutions to emulate. Unless the benefits of science and technology were taken to the villages, the country could not eradicate poverty, ignorance and diseases. The setting up of VRCs was another venture taken up by the ISRO with the MSSRF to benefit the rural society.

As Dr. Singh watched from the capital, a wide range of interactions took place between the experts at the MSSRF, Chennai and farmers and fishermen in the villages. This satellite-based project, ISRO-MSSRF-VRC, aims for digital connectivity to remote villages for providing services such as tele-medicine, tele-education and remote sensing applications through a single window.

Gandhimathi, a 37-year-old agricultural labourer in Tiruvaiyaru near Thanjavur, began complaining of breathlessness about four months ago. "I could not work. I was finding it difficult to go through every day chores," she said. Today, she consulted a specialist in Chennai—without stepping out of her village. The cardiologist wanted to see her echocardiogram and this was instantly flashed on the screen from Tiruvaiyaru. Dr. Thanikachalam confirmed his defective value and reassured Gandhimathi: "There is nothing to worry about. You don't need surgery. The medicines that we give will suffice," he told her in Tamil. The interaction was part of a live demonstration of the on-ground effectiveness of the VRCs located at Tiruvaiyaru in Thanjavur district, Thankatchimadam in Ramanathapuram district and Sempatti in Dindigul district and the MSSRF and SRMC in Chennai.

—*Courtesy*: *The Hindu*, October 19, 2004

HELPING THE VILLAGER

IT and Space Promise Benefits

Developments in information technology and India's space programmes would be meaningless if they didn't bring benefits to the millions struggling for a living in rural areas. Thankfully, these benefits have begun trickling down, with a smart beginning made in Tamil Nadu on October 18. As Prime Minister Manmohan Singh watched over a video link from New Delhi, three villages were linked to Chennai in a joint project of the Indian Space Research Organisation (ISRO) and the M.S. Swaminathan Research Foundation (MSSRF). The Village Resource Centre (VRC) concept has been developed by ISRO to give villagers relevant information using computers and satellite-based connectivity. ISRO plans to set up 100 such integrated village resource centres by the year-end in Tamil Nadu, Karnataka and some north-east states.

The VRCs are likely to include modules to help villagers participate in adult literacy programmes, monitor the weather in a way relevant to them, and give village artisans a transparent way to sell their products. Later, the centres could also take to the village level a tele-medicine project that ISRO has set up by linking major hospitals in cities to some district health centres. According to ISRO chairman G. Madhavan Nair, Government agencies do not have information on soil moisture content in a particular village where crops might be grown. The VRCs will help villagers gather that information so that agriculture scientists can advise them what to grow.

In Tamil Nadu, the MSSRF project will promote single-window delivery of need-based services in the education, health, nutrition, weather, environment, agriculture and livelihood. MSSRF has launched a project called Mission 2007 with the aim of making every village a knowledge centre to promote rural prosperity. MSSRF's project was started in 1998 in three Pondicherry villages, and results so far are said to be encouraging. The basic idea appears to have caught on, and companies like ITC and Hindustan Lever also have launched their projects to empower villages. The task of covering all six lakh villages in the country is gigantic, but with a beginning already made and support from companies and the government, it should be possible to cover them in a few years. Other than MSSRF, several organisations have taken initiatives to go beyond not just their laboratories but to the rural hinterland as well. TCS is separately involved in a computer-aided literacy programme in some Tamil Nadu districts, and plans to expand it.

Courtesy: The New Indian Express, October 30, 2004

9

The Virtual Village: Some Case Studies

S.S. JEEVAN

POWER OF INFORMATION TECHNOLOGY

Fifty six-year-old Kuppu walks up to the Internet cage near his house. He logs on to the local web site to check out his property and tax-records. He's also pleased that the computer confirms the electricity bills he paid a few days ago. To his relief, all information is in his local language. He then spots his neighbour in the cage. "Critical information on the procurement price of rice has made me a smart, rich farmer," he gushes.

Before logging out Kuppu goes through the financial records of his area. They are updated regularly and every rupees spent is accounted for. And Panchayat meetings are beamed live on the local cable channel. "Governance was never this transparent and accountable," he says. Kuppu is a villager from Belandure, located some 25 km from Bangalore. Like Kuppu, more than 10,000 people across five villages that come under Belandur Panchayat, now taste the power of information technology.

Something magical is happening in India's villages. Information Technology (IT) which was once dismissed by cynics as only benefiting the urban elite—is fast becoming a developmental tool for India's villagers. From fisherfolk getting vital information on weather alerts in Pondicherry, to shrimp farmers in Andhra Pradesh checking out global price fluctuation, the World Wide Web is touching the lives of villages across India.

VIRTUAL VILLAGES

Take for instance Anand in Gujarat, the cradle of India's cooperative have changed the way they do business. The buzzword is not high-productivity, but efficiency. The computerised automatic milk collection system allow the reading of milk quantity and quality (for fat content). It also maintains daily records of milk societies at the village level.

In the previous manual system, two to three days were spent on collecting information on the quality and quantity of milk deposited by each member. Payments were worked out manually, which consumed a lot of time. The producer was sometimes paid 10 days after depositing the milk. Now more than 200 members can deposit milk within one hour. A similar initiative is successfully running in Baramati in Maharashtra.

Punjab has gone one step further. Farmers like Kirpal Singh check out the price movements of wheat in the international market before selling. This gives Kirpal and millions of farmers a trend of the future prices of wheat in the local market. In neighbouring Haryana. farmers are using the Net for advice and purchasing better yielding seed varieties.

THE VILLAGE MARKET

The Village Market is still largely untapped. Some companies have realised this:

- ITC: The leader of the pack. ITC's Rs. 12,000 crore e-choupal is Corporate India's biggest foray into rural India. Analysts believe that e-choupal has all the makings of becoming the benchmark for rural empowerment. Already 35 companies have become partners in this initiative. The project provides many free services such as daily local weather forecast, advisory services and prices of crops. Farmers can now buy seeds, fertilisers and tractors or even sell their produce to ITC.
- DYNAMIX: The largest dairy company in the western state of Maharashtra has transformed Sharad Pawar's constituency Baramati. It has installed computerised and automated milk collection centres that have helped India retain its new-found position as the world's largest milk producer. Now the area's 100,000 largely illiterate dairy farmers have increased productivity and income inputs.
- MAHINDRA: The company is into contract farming and retail from farm inputs. Has around 35-odd outlets in Punjab, Haryana, Uttar Pradesh, Chattisgarh, Madhya Pradesh, Maharashtra, Tamil Nadu and Andhra Pradesh that are company intends to diversify into horticultural and export-oriented products like aromatic plants and flowers is also considering leasing and renting out tractors and other farm equipments to farmers.
- TATA: In partnership with about 15 companies such as ICICI Bank, ING Vysya Bank and State Bank of India, the Tatas are focussing on promoting urea—the flagship of Tata Chemicals. Their strategy is creating hubs in rural areas, where the revenue is set to come from sale, advisory services and service charges. Already more than 350 centres have been

created in Punjab, Haryana and western Uttar Pradesh and 200 more will be networked by December 2004. The company also offers contract farming. TCS will provide the network and software for this.

- EID PARRY: With the help of IT, the sugar major plans to expand in rural areas in Tamil Nadu to provide advisory services, information and finance schemes to farmers who supply sugar to its mill. Areas in focus include Nellikuppam sugar factory near Cuddalore.
- DCM: Their focus is on rural malls that will sell feed stocks, seeds, fertilisers, veterinary medicines and farm implements. They propose to give free technical advice on new crops and plant nutrients to farmers to forge a long-term relationship.

But these shining examples of IT-connected villages are still only a few in the larger context. Most of rural India's 600 million strong village communities remain cut-off from the wired world. These 6.4 lakh villages have pathetic infrastructure like power and telecom, poor social infrastructure like health and education and almost non-existent institutions like banking and marketing.

When US President Bill Clinton visited India in March 2000, one of the highlights of his trip was a visit to Nyala, a non-descript village in Rajasthan. His visit to the girl's school was billed as a showcase for the digital revolution sweeping India. The school has three computers and occasion provided the "knock-out" shot for the world's media. The Nyala girl's school was a part of the Rajasthan government's attempt at a "new era of e-governance" and connecting villages through Internet. When Clinton returned to the US, he narrated his Nyala experience and called for similar community computer centres all over the Mississippi delta.

The Panchayat Bhavan of Nyala, where the computer was installed for Clinton's perusal, today wears a deserted look. The computer lies in a small room under lock and key.

"It hasn't worked since that day, says a village elder. The villagers were given a temporary telephone connection for Internet, which was taken away right after Clinton's visit. The villagers applied for a telephone connection but nothing has happened. The school at Nyala has no power connection and the state electricity board remains deaf. The irony is that the main power line runs just 20 metres away.

BOTTLENECKS

Do we have the technological ability to connect villages? How much will these technologies cost? Can we afford them?

Ten years ago, India and China both had about five million telephone lines. India has about 25 million today, while China has crossed 140 million connections and is adding about 25 million connections every year. The National Telecom Policy of 1994 talked of a telephone in every village by 1997. It's 2004, and half of India's villagers are yet to see one.

So the most daunting challenge is connectivity. Telecom infrastructure in small towns and villages hardly exists. Experts believe that if India has to add 100 million telephone lines over the next seven to eight years, it would take an investment of Rs. 2,00,000 crore (if the cost per connection is estimated at Rs. 20,000)

If telecom infrastructure is poor then power supply is worse. And in villages that have power connections, supply is so irregular that computers cannot run. Experts say that India's power generation and transmission record is so poor that it cannot be expected to meet the demand of taking it to villages. Power backup using batteries is only a temporary solution. And renewable energy sources like solar energy remain expensive options.

Language is no longer a problem as computers are speaking local languages. But illiteracy cannot be overcome overnight. "Literacy is the main reason why we were able to launch successfully the e-governance project and persuade the people to cooperate", says K. Jagannath, Panchayat President of Belandur.

The biggest bottleneck is the lack of political will and imagination. The political classes need to realise that 70 percent of India live in villages, most of whom are still not logged on. If they get wired soon, there is huge political capital to be made from IT-connected villages. *Rural empowerment will follow.*

10

PURA—A Success Story

ANAND PARTHASARATHY

President Kalam's vision of taking urban technologies to rural area is being realized in a number of 'digital divide' projects. Just two hours out from Bangalore on the railway main line to Chennai, Kuppam is a two-minute halt on most trains. But that is time enough for most passengers to snatch a quick look at the posters lining the two platforms, welcoming them to Kuppam's 'inclusive' or i-community. For those who choose to alight, the contrast with other rural clusters in this southern corner of Andhra Pradesh is palpable: Neatly signposted lanes, a clean bus shelter and something one is unlikely to find anywhere else in rural India: bright read-and-yellow booths which say: 'Emergency Telephone' in Telugu and English. They are free phones supported by a wireless (802.11b) network and connect instantly to the local police, fire and hospital service.

They can also reach two other numbers: World Corps India, the voluntary agency that has been instrumental in training local entrepreneurs to set-up over 15 wireless

Internet-enable Community Information Centres (CICs) spread across the five villages or Mandals of Kuppam; and Hewlett Packard, whose adoption of Kuppam as one of the first sites of its global e-inclusion programmed of 'appropriate' Information Technology, has inspired the state government as well as a dozen private companies, charitable foundations and non-governmental agencies to come together and co-create a sustainable future for this so-called backward area, using cutting edge technologies that have largely been the preserve of urban pockets of plenty.

DIGITAL PHOTOGRAPHY

Like digital photography. Last week was a busy time for Neelamma and 15 other local women mobile photographers to the Kuppam community. Armed with Photosmart digital cameras, they 'covered' dozens of Ganesha 'nimarjan' (immersion) ceremonies, and using the field kits loaned to them by HP, converted the shots into instant colour photos using solar-powered direct photo printers and sold them at Rs. 30 a print.

On other days, they routinely, cover weddings, baby 'naming' ceremonies, bus route inaugurations, accident sites or dead cattle, for insurance companies and the occasional 'rowdy sheeter' mug shots for the police. . . . They earn anything from Rs. 750 to Rs. 2000 a month, and are currently moving from a model where HP supplies all the material and takes away Rs. 20 for every print to a more lucrative one where they just lease the camera and buy all the consumables.

The change has come because, the sudden access to doorstep photo services in Kuppam, has created a big enough market of nearby towns to stock digital printer consumables. "We want to move away from the pappad-and-pickle stereotype of employment for rural women," says Anand, Tawker, Director of HP's emerging market solutions in its e-inclusion programme, who has nurtured this initiative from day one. "We are thrilled that they are soon confidently handling technology that may seem disruptive even to hardcore professionals in the metros".

In his community kiosk in Kothaindlu village, proprietor M. Kumarswamy, has just one PC and a multi-function printer. He sells toiletries and sweets to attract the local customers than offers to cast their horoscopes using special software, at Rs. 30 a go.

He has also discovered a new and gainful use for the spare disk space on his PC: He calls it 'surakshita dakhalalu' ('electronic safe deposit locker'). Villagers usually have a hard time preserving their precious documents: birth certificates, land title deeds or 'pattas'... from the ravages of time and weather. Kumarswamy charges a onetime fee of Rs. 20 to scan and preserve the documents on his PC for as long as the customer wants. He has probably not heard the word 'demat' but his service is filling a very real need.

'TOUCH TYPEWRITING'

At the Mamidipudi Nagarjuna Social Welfare Residential School for Girls, 10 year olds crowd around a dozen PCs, learning 'touch typewriting' in Telugu, or browsing language software created by the Azim Premji Foundation, another partner in Kuppam's i-community. A single PC running Linux fuels four monitors which can work independently—not a particularly high tech application, but one that might be crucial in an environment where the cost of a single PC for a whole school, might be the hurdle.

They are the first beneficiaries of an exclusive 2 MBPS 'pipe' provided by the state government and fed from the Software Technology Park Tirupati, via fibre, to all five mandals of Kuppam. From here, a WiFi umbrella set-up by Convergent Communications, Bangalore, unfurls over the whole community of 3.2 lakh citizens even while fuelling the community Net portal (www.kuppamhp i-community. stph.net) that is already delivering a variety of local services under the 'Yojanalu' head. Last week, a domestic gas outlet was advertising a vacancy as were World Corps and some of the local voluntary agencies. However, the nearest government employment exchange is yet to be linked to this on-line service.

The Web for Kuppam, is also the gateway to range of health and educational services: tele-medicine software from Tele-Vital which connects remote villages to the P.E.S. Specialty Hospital and Medical College and computer-aided-education steered by World Links and the America-India foundation; documenting farm land productivity, using remote sensing satellite date collated by 7 Samuha, a voluntary agency.

On Friday last, Kuppam's i-community mobile van was parked in Vasanadu village. Local residents brought soil samples for immediate testing in the field lab even as others queued up to have their eyes tested for a possible referral to the Arvind Eye Hospital. And a crowd of school children waited to take possession of a laptop computer – their weekly treat.

This was my third visit to Kuppam since the inception of the i-community project 30 months ago. The mobile lab was new this time and so was one sight that I found most thrilling: The sight of four young local students, in small room, each in front of a PC, editing scanned images mailed from a U.S. state's Vehicle Licensing Department, filtering them through on OmniPage character recognition engine and painstakingly licking them into shape as Acrobat PDF files.

The job has been farmed out to them by Datamation, and Indian BPO player, which had the vision to share some of its work with this rural reach. The kids were proud of what they were doing: putting Kuppam on the world BPO map with its own 4 seater IT Enabled Services Centre. Now, one saw why they needed 2 MBPS on the Internet backbone.

'THE HP WAY'

The formal experiment launched by HP, comes to an end six months from now. The company long known for "The HP Way" a less commercially motivated, more socially driven work culture, encouraged by its co-founders, has found in

Kuppam a lively laboratory for its ideas of electronically driven 'inclusion'. It is very much in the spirit of Dr. A.P.J. Abdul Kalam's favourite blueprint PURA: Programme for Urban Amenities in Rural Areas. *The challenge remains to sustain the 'inclusive' drive, even while striving to create hundreds of other Kuppams.*

Bibliography

Abdul Kalam, A.P.J. (1998): with Y.S. Rajan (1998): *India 2020: A Vision for the New Millennium,* Viking, New Delhi.

——, (2002): *Ignited Minds Unleashing the Power within India,* Penguin Books, New Delhi.

——, (2002): *Ignited Minds Unleashing the Power within India,* Penguin Books, New Delhi.

——, (2002): *Ignited Minds Unleashing the Power within India,* Penguin Books, New Delhi.

Abdul Kalam, A.P.J. with Sivathanu Pillai (2004): *Envisioning an Empowered Nation: Technology for Societal Transformation,* Tata McGraw Hill, New Delhi.

Abdul Kalam, A.P.J. with Sivathanu Pillai (2004): *Envisioning an Empowered Nation: Technology for Societal Transformation,* Tata McGraw Hill, New Delhi.

Abdul Kalam, A.P.J. with Sivathanu Pillai (2004): *Envisioning an Empowered Nation: Technology for Societal Transformation,* Tata McGraw Hill, New Delhi.

Abdul Kalam, A.P.J. with Y.S. Rajan (1998): *India 2020: A Vision for the New Millennium,* Viking, New Delhi.

Abdul Kalam, A.P.J. with Y.S. Rajan (1998): *India 2020: A Vision for the New Millennium,* Viking, New Delhi.

Anand Parthasarathy (2004): "Enabling India's Rural Reaches", Science/Technology Section, *The Hindu,* September, 30.

Debraj Ray (1998): *Development Economics,* Oxford University Press, Delhi.

Ganguli, B.N. (1977): *Indian Economic Thought Nineteenth Century Perspectives,* Tata McGraw Hill, New Delhi.

Indiresan P.V. (2002): "Vision 2020: The Connectivity Mantra," *The Hindu-Business Line,* July 29.

——, (2003): "Vision 2020—Dwelling in Malady", *The Hindu-Business Line,* November 3.

——, (2003): "Vision 2020—PURA and the Government Input," *The Hindu-Business Line,* October, 20

——, (2003): "Vision 2020—The President's Dream", *The Hindu-Business Line,* August 25.

——, (2003): "Vision 2020—Urban Amenities, Rural Ambience", *The Hindu-Business Line,* October, 6

——, (2003): "Vision 2020: Making Rural India Magnetic", *The Hindu-Business Line,* July 28.

——, (2004): "Vision 2020: PURA-HUDCO Opens the Door", *The Hindu-Business Line,* November, 2004

——, (2004): *Vision 2020: What India can be, and How to Make that Happen,* ICFAI University Press, Hyderabad.

——, (2002): "Vision 2020: Dr. Kalam's Six-Point Plan", *The Hindu-Business Line,* July 15.

——, (2002): "Vision 2020: The Connectivity Mantra", *The Hindu-Business Line,* July 29.

——, (2003): "Vision 2020"—Making Rural India Magnetic", *The Hindu-Business Line,* July 28.

Jeevan, S.S. (2004): "Will the System Work?", *The New Sunday Express,* October 10

Jegadish Gandhi, P. (2004): *The Socio-Economic Thoughts of A.P.J. Abdul Kalam,* Vellore Institute of Development Studies, Vellore.

Jhingan, M.L. (2003): *The Economics of Development and Planning,* Vrinda Publications, Delhi 36th Revised Edition.

List of President's Speeches, July 25, 2002—December 29, 2003: www.presidentofindia.nic.in

List of President's Speeches, July 25, 2002—December 29, 2003: www.presidentofindia.nic.in

Report of the Committee on *India Vision 2020,* under the Chairmanship of S.P. Gupta, Planning Commission, Government of India, 2002, Academic Foundation, New Delhi, (2003).

Ruddar Datt and Sundharam, K.P.M. (2004): "PURA—A Neo-Gandhian Approach to Development," *Indian Economy,* 50th Golden Jubilee Edition, S. Chand & Co., New Delhi.

Ruddar Datt (2004): "PURA: Bridging the Rural–Urban Divide", *The Hindu-Business Line,* April 21.

Satya Sundaram, I. (2002): *Rural Development,* Himalaya Publication House, Mumbai.

Srinivasan, G. (2003): "Development via IT Road", *The Hindu-Business Line,* November 25.

Swaminathan, M.S. (2004): "Connecting Rural India", *The Hindu,* October 18.

Swaminathan, M.S., "Networked Village Resource Centre Project Launched," *The Hindu,* October 19, 2004

Venkatasubramanian, K. (2002): *An Approach Paper on India's Development on Knowledge Society,* The Centenarian Trust, Chennai.

——, (2004): Keynote Address at "the High Level Meeting to discuss PURA Scheme", Shrimati Indira Gandhi College, Tiruchirapalli, March 18.

Vipen Kapur, (2000): *Power Through Peoples and Principles, Not Puppets and Prejudices,* McGraw-Hill, Malayasia.

Index

By the Same Author

The Socio-Economic Thoughts of A.P.J. Abdul Kalam

"Dr. A.P.J. Abdul Kalam has come as a messiah to lift up the downtrodden by his unique Social-Economic thinking...........this very fine book on an excellent person."

—*Dr. K. Venkatasubarmanian*, former Member, Union Planning Commission.

"I found it (book) very interesting."

—*Dr. P.V. Indiresan*

"The cogent compilation of the speeches and thoughts of Dr. Kalam was the special feature of the book."

—*Dr. E. Balagurusamy*, Vice-Chancellor, Anna University, Chennai.

"The book is first of its kind on Dr. Kalam's Socio-Economic ideas."

—*Mr. G. Viswanathan*, Chancellor, Vellore Institute of Technology, Deemed University.

". . . an authentical and very well documented work .... a strong point is its lucidity and clarity of thought."

—*Dr. V. Loganathan*, Tagore Emeritus Professor of Economics, University of Madras.

"Putting them (Dr. Kalam's basic ideas) down systematically in a readable fashion and articulating those ideas into formal models."

—*Prof. Abdul Aziz*, in *Southern Economist*, Institute for Socio-Economic and Change, Bangalore.

". . . . weaving all the thoughts of President Abdul Kalam into a fabric of a single Volume."

—*Prof. Ruddar Datt*, Author of *Indian Economy*.

"Dr. Kalam's dynamic thoughts with visionaries has been an inspiration."

—*Mr. D. Murali*, in *The Hindu-Business Line*.

"A debate based on this book may be initiated....in all the educational institutions towards nation-building."

—*Prof. S.J.A. Packiyaraj* in *The Rally*, Chennai.

pp. xv + 174 Hard Cover Rs. 250 Students/Educational Institutions Rs. 200.

Copies can be had from: The Director, Vellore Institute of Development Studies, No. 1034/2, Phase II, Sathuvachari, Vellore 632 009, India.

Phone No: 0416 - 2252411 Fax No: 0416 - 2253116. e-mail: jegagandhi@yahoo.com